**Living and Celebrating
Our Catholic Customs and Traditions**

The Advent–
Christmas Book

Joan Marie Arbogast

Illustrated by Virginia Helen Richards, FSP

Photos by Mary Emmanuel Alves, FSP

Pauline
BOOKS & MEDIA
Boston

Library of Congress Cataloging-in-Publication Data

Arbogast, Joan Marie.
  The Advent-Christmas book / by Joan Marie Arbogast.
     p. cm. — (Living and celebrating our Catholic customs and traditions)
  ISBN 0-8198-0774-5 (pbk.)
  1. Advent. 2. Christmas. I. Title. II. Series.
  BV40.A665 2004
  263'.91—dc22

                                                    2004021637

All scripture quotations in this publication are from the *Contemporary English Version* copyright © 1991, 1992, 1995 by American Bible Society. Used by Permission.

The following first appeared in *My Friend* magazine; used with permission of the authors and illustrators:

"Three Purple, One Pink" by Sandra Humphrey, illustrated by Catherine Frey Murphy

"A Handmade Christmas" by Diana Jenkins, illustrated by Mary Rojas

"Where Are All the Smiles Now?" by Nicole M. Schoenfeld, illustrated by Chuck Galey

"Christmas Reflections" illustrated by Steve Delmonte

"Enjoy My Birthday" illustrated by Tom Kinarney

Published by Pauline Books & Media, 50 Saint Paul's Avenue, Boston, MA 02130-3491. Printed in the U.S.A.

www.pauline.org; myfriendmagazine.com

Pauline Books & Media is the publishing house of the Daughters of St. Paul, an international congregation of women religious serving the Church with the communications media.

1 2 3 4 5 6 7 8 9   11 10 09 08 07 06 05 04

Contents

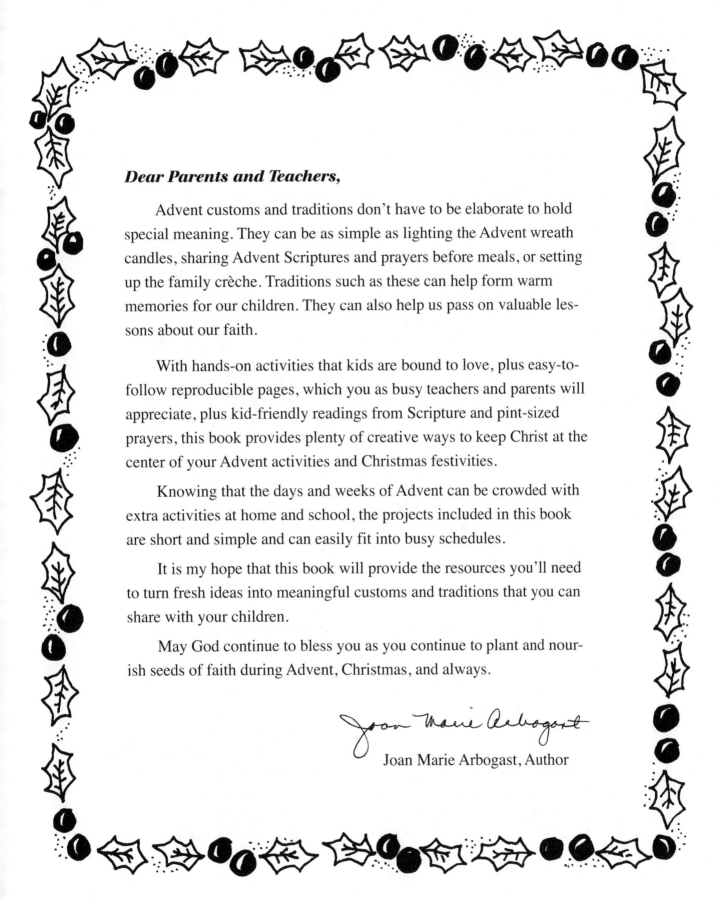

Dear Parents and Teachers,

Advent customs and traditions don't have to be elaborate to hold special meaning. They can be as simple as lighting the Advent wreath candles, sharing Advent Scriptures and prayers before meals, or setting up the family crèche. Traditions such as these can help form warm memories for our children. They can also help us pass on valuable lessons about our faith.

With hands-on activities that kids are bound to love, plus easy-to-follow reproducible pages, which you as busy teachers and parents will appreciate, plus kid-friendly readings from Scripture and pint-sized prayers, this book provides plenty of creative ways to keep Christ at the center of your Advent activities and Christmas festivities.

Knowing that the days and weeks of Advent can be crowded with extra activities at home and school, the projects included in this book are short and simple and can easily fit into busy schedules.

It is my hope that this book will provide the resources you'll need to turn fresh ideas into meaningful customs and traditions that you can share with your children.

May God continue to bless you as you continue to plant and nourish seeds of faith during Advent, Christmas, and always.

Joan Marie Arbogast, Author

How to Use this Book

The Advent-Christmas Book is designed for use by teachers, DRE's, parents, and anyone interested in living and celebrating with children traditions and symbols of the Advent and Christmas seasons. It is written for both the home and classroom setting.

Each week of Advent, the Birthday Party for Baby Jesus, and Christmas Season are separate sections as indicated by the side tabs. Over 30 reproducible activity pages are at the end of the book.

Material for each week of Advent and the the Christmas season includes: an introductory page to familiarize adults with the week's theme and activities, a story from *My Friend—a Catholic magazine for kids*, an Advent wreath ceremony for the week, a variety of crafts and activities to use with children of all ages centering on the week's theme, a family take-home page, and a customs and traditions section.

The daily, central activity for each week of Advent is the **Advent wreath ceremony.** If the book is being used at school, the Advent wreath ceremony can be photocopied each week and sent home so that this key Advent prayer-ritual can take place both at home and at school. All pages of *The Advent-Christmas Book* which include a copyright notice may be photocopied (please see copyright page at the beginning of this book).

For each week of the Advent-Christmas season, there are **craft** and **gift** ideas, and **kitchen fun** recipes for various ages. Activities which are appropriate for younger children are marked *Easy*. To make your templates for any activity a little sturdier, consider making them out of card stock or cardboard. All activities are easily adaptable for children of different ages, so feel free to be creative with the suggestions given in this book to make them appropriate for your group.

The five stories taken from *My Friend* magazine can be either read aloud to the children for discussion or can be left in a learning center for children to read and later journal on their reflection of the story. The last story titled "Enjoy my Birthday—A Letter from Jesus" has a short prayer exercise which children can either do on their own or the prayer can be led by an adult.

The **Family Take-Home Pages** found in each week can also strengthen the home-school connection. These pages can also be sent home at the beginning of the week so that families have time to plan the evenings they will incorporate the activities suggested on the page. The activities and prayer experiences on these pages are multi-age appropriate and are intended to be integrated over time.

The **Family Customs and Traditions** pages contained at the end of each section are intended to help families re-discover the richness of established family traditions and open the possibility of incorporating new customs into how they celebrate the Advent and Christmas season.

On page 93, you will find everything you need to throw a **Baby Jesus Birthday Party**. It is recommended that, if you would like to have this party, you should begin to plan for it early in the Advent season.

Have a very blessed and holy Advent and Christmas seasons.

About Advent

In class we are learning about Advent: its meaning and symbols. Below you will find helpful information about Advent including information about the Advent wreath, which we will be using at school and we encourage you to use at home.

Advent marks the beginning of the Church calendar year. It starts on the Sunday following the Solemnity of Christ the King (a Sunday at the end of November or beginning of December) and ends Christmas Eve with the celebration of the Vigil Mass.

During the four weeks of Advent we commemorate the coming of Jesus to Bethlehem more than 2,000 years ago; we prepare for his final coming at the end of the world; and we celebrate his coming into our hearts today.

In a spirit of anxious anticipation we prepare once again, with grateful hearts, to celebrate the coming of Jesus, our Savior and Lord.

The most common symbol for Advent is the Advent wreath. Its circular shape, formed by evergreens, is a symbol of eternal life. Its three purple candles symbolize our time of waiting, our time of repenting, our time of preparing for the Lord. Its pink candle represents a time for rejoicing as we move closer to Christmas. The light cast from the candles reminds us of Jesus, the Light of the World.

For many families, the Advent wreath also serves as a centerpiece for the dining room table. As they gather for meals, the wreath provides a visual reminder that Jesus is the reason for their coming celebrations.

Advent wreath ceremonies combine the lighting of the Advent wreath candles with readings from Scripture plus songs and/or prayers. The Scripture readings speak of watching, waiting, and hoping; they speak of preparing and living at peace; they speak of rejoicing and light; and they speak of love and the coming of the Lord.

Advent wreath ceremonies provide wonderful opportunities for communal prayer, whether they're held with family members before meals, over the PA system at school, with classmates gathered around the prayer table at religious education classes, or with parishioners at daily Mass. With Scripture readings, simple prayers, and lit candles, a meaningful tradition is handed on to the next generation of faith.

Each week of Advent, your child will bring home a handout similar to this one. The handout will include the Scripture readings, prayers, and songs for that particular week to use in your home Advent wreath ceremony. I encourage you to use the ceremony as a time for your family to come together and share our faith.

Symbols are a part of tradition.

Traditions are a part of faith.

Sincerely,

_____
(Teacher's signature)

First Week of Advent

The main theme for the first week of Advent is that of watchful waiting; the secondary theme is that of hope.

Tools for marking our days of Advent (the Advent wreath and Advent calendar) are presented in Week One. Both the wreath and calendar serve as symbols that remind us that Jesus is at the center of our longing and waiting. Because the wreath will be used in our daily Advent wreath ceremony, directions for making one are found on page 15.

As with all the weeks of Advent, it is a good idea to glance through each section ahead of time so you are familiar with the various activities. Some activities, such as the Advent wreath or calendar, will require advance planning in order to collect supplies and make items, which will be used throughout the season.

Make sure to flip to the back of the book (starting on page 115) where you will find reproducible puzzles and games.

Week-at-a-Glance

Three Purple, O

By Sandra Humphrey
Illustrated by Catherine Frey Murphy

Advent is my favorite time of year! And not just because I know Christmas is coming and I'll get some cool presents.

Advent is the four weeks before Christmas when our family pulls out the box marked "Advent" and puts the Advent wreath together. My mom says that the wreath is a great way not only to celebrate Jesus' birth, but to make our hearts truly ready to receive him.

Right now she's got all the stuff laid out on the dining room table, and even my little brother Noah is excited.

"Ben, come here!" he yells. "We're doing the Jesus wreath."

Our Advent wreath has four candles arranged in a circle-three purple and one pink. The three purple candles symbolize hope, peace, and love, and we light those candles on the first, second, and fourth Sundays of Advent. The pink candle symbolizes joy and we light that one on the third Sunday.

As I help my mom lay the little evergreen branches around the four candles, I can smell the pine scent and it smells really good. Mom says that the evergreen branches and the circular shape of the Advent wreath symbolize eternal life.

And then, right in the middle of the wreath, we always put a white candle. We call it the Christ candle because it symbolizes the birth of Jesus, and we light that one on Christmas day.

During Advent we eat only by the light of the candles, which I think is really cool. My dad always says a little prayer as he lights the candles. Noah loves to blow the candles out at the end of the meal.

The first week when we light only one purple candle, there is not a whole lot of light, but the second week we

Pink

Then the fourth week we light all four candles and there is a lot of light. On Christmas Day we light the white Christ candle and that's when I get my goose bumps. It's like Jesus is right there celebrating his birth with us.

After we finish making our Advent wreath, I'm upstairs lying on my bed just thinking, when I hear something strange coming from my brother's room next door.

I quietly open his door just far enough to peek in. I see him sitting there on his Lion King rug with tears streaming down his cheeks.

"So how's it going, big guy?" I ask, as I plop myself down on the rug next to him. "What are we trying to do here?"

He points to the colored construction paper and magic markers in front of him as more tears flow. "I'm trying to make the Jesus wreath like Mommy, but I can't do it."

"Not to worry," I tell him as I remember back to my first grade Sunday school class with Mrs. Emerson. "I know what we can do."

I rush down to the basement where Mom keeps all kinds of craft supplies and grab four small cardboard rolls (the kind that come from toilet paper) and one large one that came from paper towels. On my way through the kitchen, I grab a large paper plate.

get to light two purple candles and then there is a little more light.

By the third week, when we light the pink candle, there is a lot more light. My dad says that the pink candle is a different color from the rest because it symbolizes Light overcoming darkness. When the first two candles are lit, there are still two unlit candles, but when the third candle is lit, Light wins!

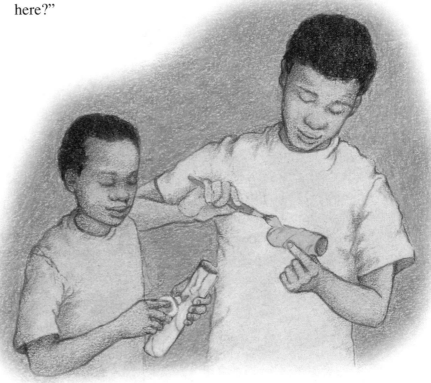

First Week of Advent

Then I grab some yellow tissue paper from my mom's stock of gift wrap and some old newspapers from the recycling bin on the back porch. I find the white glue and the paint set in my desk.

"Okay, guy, we're all ready to go," I tell Noah, as I plop down next to him with all my stuff and lay out the old newspapers all over his Lion King rug.

I notice Noah's tears have stopped flowing. Even though my brother has no idea what we're doing, he is faithfully following my instructions. Kind of like the way I trust Mom and Dad when I do what they tell me to do even though I don't always know why I'm doing it.

The first step is to paint the toilet paper rolls. Noah loves this. He sloshes purple paint on three toilet paper rolls while I paint the fourth one pink. Then I trim a little off the top of the paper towel roll and paint it white.

While the paint is drying on the cardboard rolls, I trim off a few little branches from one of our evergreen bushes in the front yard. These will go around the edge of the paper plate.

Then we drip some of the glue down the sides of the paper towel roll and toilet paper rolls and let it dry. Right now it just looks like globs of glue, but later I know it will look like melting wax.

While we're waiting for everything to dry, Noah settles in my lap while I read one of his "Curious George" books to him. And I wonder if this is how God feels when we spend time with him in prayer and just talk to him about our day.

When everything is dry, we glob some glue on the bottoms of all five cardboard rolls and stick them on the paper plate in a circle with the white paper towel roll in the middle. Then I rearrange the evergreen branches around the "candles" while Noah's eyes get as big as silver dollars.

"We did it, we did it! My own Jesus wreath!"

"Not yet, buddy," I tell him, as I begin cutting up the yellow tissue paper. "We have one more thing to do."

I stuff gold tissue paper into the cardboard rolls and then pull it up just enough to "light" our candles. Noah's eyes light up even brighter than the candles on the paper plate, and he wraps his arms around me in a tight hug.

I don't have any idea what I'm getting for Christmas, but I think maybe Noah has just given me my best Christmas gift ever!

Reprinted from *My Friend—A Catholic Magazine for Kids*, Pauline Books & Media, 50 Saint Pauls Avenue, Boston, MA 02130. www.myfriendmagazine.com

Making An Advent Wreath

The Advent wreath is a visual reminder of this special time of the liturgical year. If you don't already have one, why not make one? It's as easy as one, two, three! If working with younger children, make the wreath as described in *Three Purple, One Pink* on page 12.

Supplies needed:

permanent marker

circular Styrofoam™ base

garland of silk greens

florist wire

wire cutters or old scissors

3 purple candles

1 pink candle

1 yard of narrow, pink ribbon (optional)

3 yards of narrow, purple ribbon (optional)

Directions:

1. With permanent marker, mark 4 "Xs" on Styrofoam™ ring, equal distances apart. ("Xs" mark where candles will stand.)

2. To form holes for candles, twist and turn candle into Styrofoam™ base, applying pressure as you twist and turn. Form four holes for the candles, but do not leave candles standing in place. They will be added after greens are wired to base.

3. Wrap garland of silk greens around Styrofoam™ base, covering outside, top, and inside of base. Leave bottom of Styrofoam™ free of greens.

4. Secure greens with florist wire, wrapping wire around Styrofoam™ base. Use wire cutters or old scissors to cut wire. Tie ends of wire together to keep wire secure.

5. Place candles in holes.

6. (Optional) Tie ribbons to candles for festive look.

Reflection

God desires to make his love tangible through you. God wants you to be his hands, his feet, his smile—so that he can touch the lives of your children and friends through you.

—*Sr. Ancilla Christine Hirsch, FSP*

1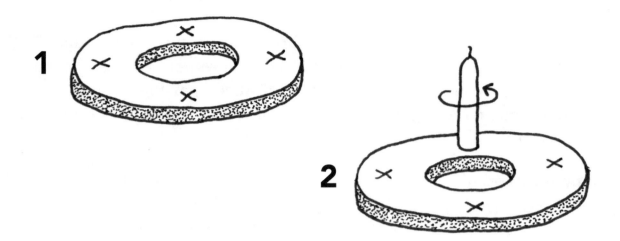

2

3

4

5

Advent Wreath Ceremony

The Advent wreath symbolizes our time of waiting, our time of hoping. It helps us mark our days until Christmas.

The Advent wreath ceremony provides you with an opportunity to pass on tradition, to share Scripture and prayer, and to help children understand that Christ is at the center of our days of waiting.

The ceremony takes only minutes, making it easy to incorporate into busy days. One person reads the Scripture passage, another reads the prayer, another lights the candle, then everyone joins in with the response. While the candle is lit, remember not to leave it unattended. When you have finished gathering around the Advent wreath extinguish the flame.

Romans 13:11

It is time to wake up. You know that the day when we will be saved is nearer now than when we first put our faith in the Lord.

Reader:

Heavenly Father,
on this the first Sunday of Advent,
we begin to mark the days
until the birthday of your Son.
As we light this first purple candle,
we think of Jesus,
our Hope for the world.
May we, as followers of Jesus,
bring hope to a waiting world.
Amen.

Light first purple candle.

All:

Come, Jesus, Hope for the world.
Come, Lord Jesus, come.

Mark 13:32–33

No one knows the day or the time. The angels in heaven don't know, and the Son himself doesn't know. Only the Father knows. So watch out and be ready!

Reader:

Lord God,
we are so anxious for Christmas!
We have already started
to count down the days!

Please help us spend these days
of anxious waiting
with kind deeds
and gentle words.
Amen.

Light first purple candle.

All:

Come, Jesus, Hope for the world.
Come, Lord Jesus, come.

Week 1
TUE

Romans 15:12

Isaiah says, "Someone from David's family will come to power. He will rule the nations, and they will put their hope in him."

Reader:

Heavenly Father,
your prophet Isaiah
encouraged our ancestors
to place their hope
and trust in you.
Help us learn to trust in you always—
we know that you
will never let us down.
Amen.

Light first purple candle.

All:

Come, Jesus, Hope for the world.
Come, Lord Jesus, come.

Week 1
WED

Psalm 130:5

*With all my heart,
I am waiting, LORD, for you!
I trust your promises.*

Song:

(Sung to the tune: "London Bridge Is Falling Down." Leader sings once, then everyone joins in.)

I am waiting for the Lord,
for the Lord,
for the Lord.
I am waiting for the Lord.
Come, Lord Jesus.

(Additional verses could include: I am hoping in... I am trusting in....)

Light first purple candle.

All:

Come, Jesus, Hope for the world.
Come, Lord Jesus, come.

Psalm 25:4–5

Show me your paths

and teach me to follow; guide me by your truth

and instruct me.

You keep me safe, and I always trust you.

Reader:

> With all my heart
> and with all my soul
> I trust in you,
> my Lord and my God.
> Amen.

> *Light first purple candle.*

All:

> Come, Jesus, Hope for the world.
> Come, Lord Jesus, come.

Daniel 12:12

God will bless everyone who patiently waits....

Reader:

> Dear Lord,
> sometimes I'm not very patient.
> Sometimes I want what I want
> Right now!
> Please help me grow
> in your patience, Lord,

as I wait for Christmas
to come.
Amen.

> *Light first purple candle.*

All:

> Come, Jesus, Hope for the world.
> Come, Lord Jesus, come.

1 Thessalonians 3:12–13

May the Lord make your love for each other and for everyone else grow by leaps and bounds.... And when our Lord comes with all of his people, I pray that he will make your hearts pure and innocent in the sight of God the Father.

Reader:

> Sweet Jesus,
> while we pass
> these days of Advent
> waiting for Christmas to come,
> help us grow to be more patient,
> help us to grow in faith,
> hope and love.
> Thank you, sweet Jesus.
> Amen.

> *Light first purple candle.*

All:

> Come, Jesus, Hope for the world.
> Come, Lord Jesus, come.

A Tree-Full-of-Love Banner

This simple banner helps children mark the passing days of Advent with symbols of love for Jesus, the Light of the World.

Supplies needed:

1/2 yard of 45" wide navy blue felt

1/2 yard of 45" wide green felt

1 pre-cut 8" x 11" piece of red felt

1 pre-cut 8" x 11" piece of white felt

1 dowel rod, 1/4" diameter, 16" long

1 yard ribbon

scissors

craft glue or stapler

pen or marker

Directions:

1. Cut 14 inch by 23 inch rectangle from navy blue felt.

2. Cut out templates.

3. Copy tree template on pages 22–23. Cut out tree template. Assemble tree by taping both halves of the tree to form the whole tree. Trace the tree template onto green felt with marker or pen. Cut tree from felt.

4. Place the blue felt rectangle on work surface so that rectangle measures 14 inches wide and 23 inches long. Glue tree to navy blue felt.

5. Trace enough hearts for each day of Advent onto red felt. Cut out hearts.

6. Trace star template onto white felt. Cut out star.

7. To form casing for dowel, fold top of navy blue rectangle down 1 inch. Glue or staple casing into place.

8. Slide dowel through casing. Dowel will extend 1 inch beyond casing at either end.

9. Tie ribbon to dowel ends. Hang banner by ribbon on wall or door for all to see.

10. Have family members or students take turns placing one heart on the banner with each passing day of Advent. There is no need to glue hearts onto banner. The hearts will cling to the felt like a flannel board.

Teachers: Make these with your students and then send them home with page 30.

Paper Chain Advent Calendar

Easy

Help little ones count down the days of Advent with this simple paper chain.

Supplies needed:

construction paper: brown, yellow, white, purple, and pink

scissors

glue

ruler

pens, markers, or pencils

notebook paper

Directions:

1. Photocopy templates on pages 24–25 and cut them out.

2. Trace templates onto construction paper then cut: manger and small oval from brown construction paper, halo and hay (combined piece) from yellow construction paper, the baby wrapped in swaddling clothes from white construction paper.

3. Glue halo/hay onto manger.

4. Draw eyes and smile on small brown oval. Glue face onto swaddling clothes. (Do not glue baby Jesus onto the hay until Christmas morning.)

5. With ruler and pencil, measure and mark 1 by 7 inch strips on pink and purple construction paper. Cut 14 purple strips for the first two weeks of Advent, 7 pink strips for the third week, plus enough purple strips for the last week. (Check your calendar because the number of days in the fourth week of Advent changes every year.)

6. Enlist the help of your family or students. Have them suggest "good deeds" that can be done during Advent and write one deed on each of the strips.

7. Form first "link" of chain by stapling or gluing ends of one purple strip together. The "good deed" should be hidden inside "link."

8. Add 13 more purple "links" (for the first two weeks of Advent), then 7 pink "links" for the third week, then the rest of the purple "links" for the fourth week.

9. Staple paper chain to manger. (Make sure to staple the last purple "link" from the fourth week to the manger, otherwise your color-coded "links" won't match up to your weeks.)

10. Number each "link" starting with the one attached to the manger. (This way it helps you "count down" your days.)

11. Hang manger for all to see. Remove one "link" each day during Advent and read the "good deed" to your class or family. Encourage them to secretly perform the "good deed" sometime during the day. Day after day the chain will shorten; soon Christmas will be here!

Teachers: Make these with your students and send them home with page 31.

The Advent–Christmas Book

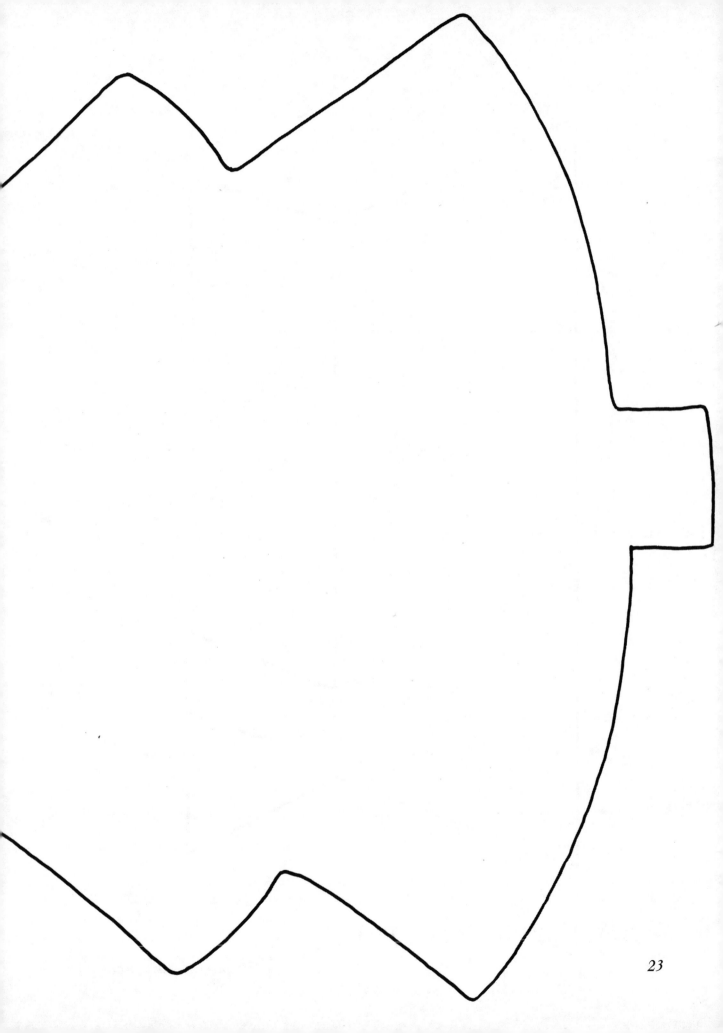

23

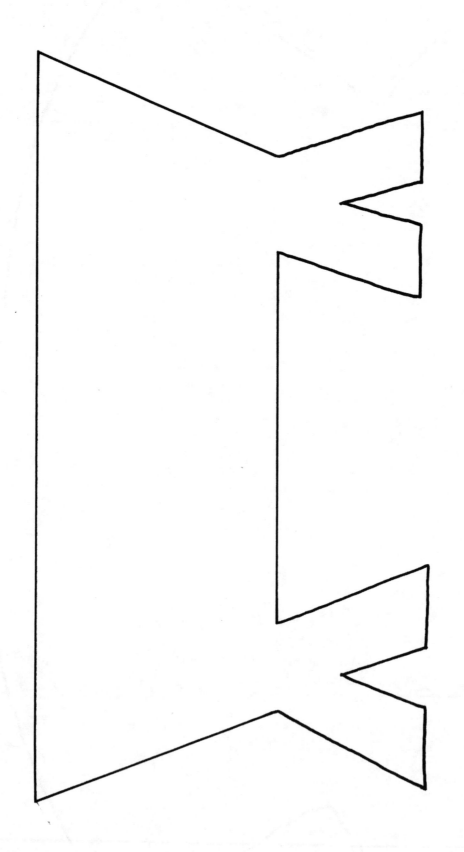

The Advent–Christmas Book

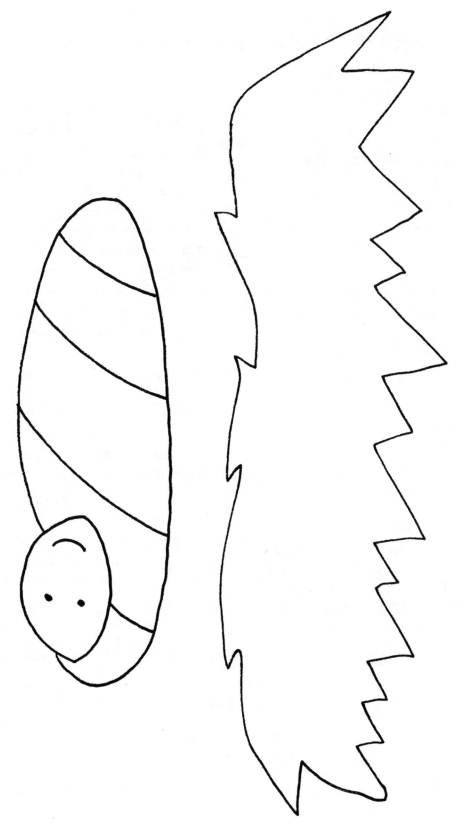

First Week of Advent

Rocking Angel

This angel rocks! It makes a great gift and a heavenly decoration for any room.

Supplies needed:

  paper plate (Any size will do. If you are
    working with small children the
    bigger the plate the better.)
  construction paper (multi-cultural
    colors like brown, tan, yellow, red)
  glitter
  markers
  yarn (either yellow, red, brown or black)
  5" piece of chenille wire (pipe cleaner),
    either yellow, gold, or white
  1" x 2" piece of cardboard
  1" x 2 1/2" piece of cardboard
  ribbon
  white craft glue
  masking tape
  scissors

Directions:

1. Fold paper plate in half.

2. Using a pastic or paper drinking cup trace a circle onto construction paper or use a cardboard template about 2 1/2 inches in diameter. Cut out the circle. This will be the head and face of the angel.

3. With markers, have the children draw the angel's face on one side of the circle.

4. Have child pick yarn for the angel's hair. With masking tape attach one end of yarn to either 1 inch by 2 inch piece of cardboard or the 1 inch by 2 1/2 inch piece of cardboard (depending on desired length of hair). Wrap yarn around the cardboard 4 or 5 times. Cut yarn from skein. Holding yarn to the cardboard, cut yarn at both ends of the cardboard.

5. Glue yarn on head. Glue bottom of circle to plate in the center of the fold. See illustration.

6. Drizzle glue on front side of plate and sprinkle with glitter. Let glue dry. To help it dry faster, a hair dryer can be used on the lowest setting.*

7. Once glue dries, drizzle glue on the back side of the plate and sprinkle with glitter. Let glue dry.

8. Form a small bow from ribbon and glue below angel's face.

9. Form "halo" with chenille wire and slide over angel's head. It's not necessary to glue "halo."

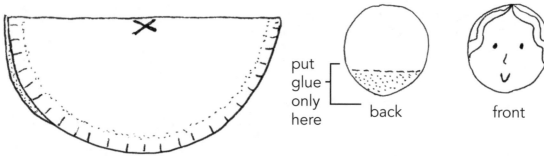

put
glue
only
here

back

front

While children are waiting for the glue and glitter to dry they can make a card for the person who will receive the gift.

A Card of Encouragement

It is important for children to know that they too are called to be witnesses to Christ. A card of encouragement allows children to take the responsibility of praying for others as a very special mission and gift to people they know. This card will also teach children the value of non-material gifts, which they can give to others.

Supplies needed:

construction paper

pencil

scissors

markers, pens, crayons

Bibles

Directions:

1. Fold a sheet of construction paper in half.

2. Have the child trace his/her left hand, fingers together, along the fold as shown.

3. Cut along the outline of the hand. DO NOT cut along fold.

4. Have the child think of someone who could use the gift of prayer. Write the person's name on the front of the hand-shaped card.

5. Open the card and write on the left side: I am praying for you.

6. Have the children look through their Bibles to find an appropriate verse for what they want to say, or suggest some verses to the children. On the right side, write the encouraging verse from the Bible and/or a personal message to the person.

    For young children: instead of writing a Bible verse they can "sign" their name on the left below the "I am praying for you." On the right side the child can draw a picture.

7. Set aside a few minutes each day during which the children can pray for this person.

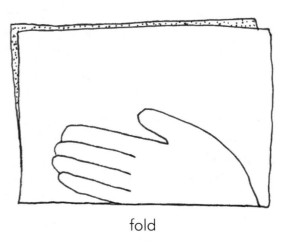

fold

Reflection

"St. John the Baptist invites us all to return to God, decisively fleeing sin, which infests the human heart and causes a person to lose the joy of meeting the Lord. The Advent season is particularly apt for experiencing God's saving love. It is especially through the sacrament of Reconciliation that Christians can experience this, rediscovering the truth of their own existence in the light of God's word, and tasting the joy of being once more at peace with themselves and God."

—*John Paul II*

Traditions create memories. Memories enrich our lives. Traditions also help us pass on valuable lessons to our children and to our children's children.

Setting Up the Crèche

Saint Francis of Assisi is credited with creating the first live nativity scene in Greccio, Italy, back in 1223. Live animals and children were a part of the scene. Since then, the custom of displaying a crèche during the Advent and Christmas seasons has become a treasured tradition for families the world over.

The custom of setting up your crèche can begin to unfold on the first Sunday of Advent and continue until Christmas Eve.

On the first Sunday of Advent the family gathers to unveil the stable. The stable is empty; it is bleak. It is not ready to welcome the newborn Prince of Peace.

During the Advent season, the family gathers daily around the stable while one person adds a figurine to the scene. Often a prayer is said, a song is sung, or a passage from Scripture is read. If you don't have enough figurines to place one at the scene per day, then other decorations like straw, stones, miniature shrubs and trees, or fake snow can be used. Little by little, day by day, the family prepares the stable for the coming Christ child. On Christmas Eve the last piece, the infant Jesus, is placed in the stable.

In addition to setting up the family crèche, some parents give miniature nativity sets to their children so they can display them in their bedrooms on dressers or night stands, or nestle them among the branches of the Christmas tree. These inexpensive sets can be purchased at most Christian gift shops. They

come with tiny figures already glued into place, a star stuck to a glittery roof, and a hole where a hook can be inserted so they can be hung on a tree. Ideally these sets are placed near tree lights so they are awash with the light from above.

Some families even choose to participate in live nativities sponsored by local churches, much the same as St. Francis did many centuries ago.

Whether families choose to participate in live nativity scenes, set up a family crèche, or

Reflection

"The gift is certain, because God is already pledged, already in our world, already Emmanuel. We are irrevocably, unconditionally loved."

—*Maria Boulding*

nestle miniature nativities among the branches of the tree, the message remains the same. Jesus, the Light of the World, is at the center of our Advent activities and hopefully at the center of all that we do.

Advent Calendars

Advent calendars come in all shapes and sizes. They help us count down the days until Christmas. They remind us that time is quickly fleeting.

The most common Advent calendars are the ones with colorful scenes mass-produced on card-quality paper. These detailed scenes have 24 pre-cut shuttered windows. Each window is assigned a number, starting with 1 and ending with 24. Starting on December 1, one window is opened to reveal a hidden detail or verse from Scripture. The final one is opened on Christmas Eve. Our time of waiting ends and the celebration begins!

Some Advent calendars are actually banners with 24 numbered pockets. Inside the pockets are treats and trinkets for each day of Advent, beginning December 1.

Other calendars resemble Christmas trees made from Styrofoam™ cones or wooden slats. These trees are adorned with numbered treats to be shared on each of the days leading to Christmas, starting with the first of December.

The Advent calendar found in this book takes the shape of the traditional paper chain (page 21). If you have a preschooler, kindergartner, or first grader, you've probably seen chains made of red and green construction pa-

per. They're usually attached to a Santa centered holiday scene. With each passing day, one link is removed. As the chain shortens, anticipation heightens because Santa will soon be here!

With a few minor changes, this common custom can help young families focus on Jesus as they count down the days of until Christmas. Simply replace the Santa scene with a manger full of hay. Replace the red and green links with purple and pink links to represent the days of Advent. As each day passes, a link is removed and a kind deed (which is written inside the link) is performed as a "gift" to Jesus—the greatest gift of all. These deeds help prepare our hearts to receive Jesus on Christmas morning when Jesus is placed in the manger full of hay.

Although the "art" part of this paper link chain is easy enough for preschoolers to complete, performing the extra-special kind deeds on a daily basis may prove to be challenging for the whole family!

Reflection

Among the things I received at Christmas as a child was one gift I didn't leave behind in my childhood. This gift had no price tag, and, in fact, it could not be bought for any amount of money. It was the priceless gift of love. Love is a gift anyone can give. And more and more in these days of economic difficulty, love is a gift we need to give children.

—*Sr. Ancilla Christine Hirsch, FSP*

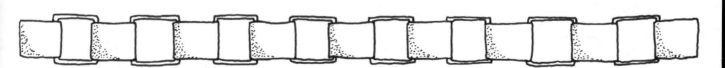

Tree-Full-of-Love Banner

Banners proclaim days worthy of celebrations like birthdays, holidays, and anniversaries. They note the four seasons, they display messages to consumers, announce community events, and honor those worthy of praise. In short, banners hold symbols and messages for all eyes that behold their designs.

They can be found in churches, public buildings, houses, and schools. Banners hang from flagpoles, lampposts, windows, and doors. They even trail from airplanes overhead.

Many cities hoist seasonal banners on lampposts along city streets. During the traditional season of Advent, these commercial banners sport reindeer and sleigh bells, snowflakes, stars, Christmas trees, candles, candy canes, and presents.

Some families design Advent banners to display inside their homes. These banners focus on the spiritual aspect of the season. Each year, as the first Sunday of Advent draws near, they search for the banner up in the attic, along with the Advent wreath and nativity set or crèche.

If you don't have an Advent banner, consider making one. The Tree-Full-of-Love Banner (page 20) provides the makings of a simple, yet meaningful custom for families. This Advent banner doubles as an Advent calendar, one that marks the passing days of Advent with tiny felt hearts. The message instilled by the custom is that Christmas is a gift of love.

With each passing day of Advent, family members take turns adding a heart to the Tree-Full-of-Love Banner. Each heart represents a gift of love to Jesus, our Savior and Lord. Each heart placed on the tree should represent a kind deed done during the day.

By Christmas Eve, the Tree-Full-of-Love Banner should be filled with gifts of love! On Christmas Eve, the star is placed at the top of the tree as a symbol of Jesus, the Light of the World—he is the perfect gift of love!

Reflection

Christmas is here again. It is the most anxiously awaited of the Church's liturgical "reruns." Every year, as any good producer, the Church schedules again her most popular programs: Advent, Christmas, Lent, Easter, etc. How many times we have rejoiced in this repeated ceremony. During the season of Advent, the Church makes present the expectancy of the people who listened to the preaching of John the Baptist: "The Lord is near!" The four weeks of Advent help us relive the centuries of waiting and longing for the Messiah. This reliving quickens our ardent desire for his second coming, "Come, Lord Jesus!" In the liturgy, the readings of the first two Sundays highlight Christ's Second Coming. The last two Sundays speak directly to the theme of God becoming man in the Incarnation, with the fourth Sunday adverting expressly to Mary, his Mother.

—Sr. Mary Lea Hill, FSP

First Week of Advent

Take-home pages offer some family activities that support what we are learning at school. We'd like you to consider choosing a few of these activities that you can share with your child and family at home.

Take one or two nights this week to share with your family the anticipation that is so much a part of the Advent season. Plan early in the week the evenings you will come together to participate in which activities.

Some of the activities call for quiet reflection; some require an activity or project, some require advance planning like gathering supplies and assembling a simple project that will be used throughout the week. Please read over the entire handout to see if advance planning is needed for any of the activities you choose to do.

Warm-Up Exercises

1. Gather the family around the Advent wreath. Have one member light the first purple candle. Ask other members of the family to take turns reading the following passage from Scripture:

When the Son of Man comes in his glory with all of his angels, he will sit on his royal throne. The people of all nations will be brought before him, and he will separate them, as shepherds separate their sheep from their goats. He will place the sheep on his right and the goats on his left. Then the king will say to those on his right, "My father has blessed you! Come and receive the kingdom that was prepared for you before the world was created. When I was hungry, you gave me something to eat, and when I was thirsty, you gave me something to drink. When I was a stranger, you welcomed me, and when I was naked, you gave me clothes to wear. When I was sick, you took care of me, and when I was in jail, you visited me." Then the ones who pleased the Lord will ask, "When did we give you something to eat or drink? When did we welcome you as a stranger or give you clothes to wear or visit you while you were sick or in jail?" The king will answer, "Whenever you did it for any of my people, no matter how unimportant they seemed, you did it for me" (Mt 25:31–40).

2. After reading the passage from Scripture, discuss with each other what you have read and what it means in your life. Below are some questions to guide your family reflection

When have we cared for the sick?

When have we fed the hungry or clothed the naked?

Have we visited someone in prison? How about someone in a nursing home or confined to bed? Aren't they imprisoned, too?

Have we welcomed new neighbors or new kids at school or new members of our parish?

No doubt, your children will be able to name quite a few times your family has helped others in need!

3. Next, have everyone close their eyes. Then tell them to think of a time when they really needed someone's help. Give them time to think before asking the following questions: How did you feel? What did you do? Who did you go to for help? How did they help you? What did it feel like when you were being helped? You can decide whether these questions are for silent reflection and

perhaps journaling or to be shared with the entire family.

Tell your children that every time we help others who are struggling, we bring them the gift of hope.

Getting Started...

As a family, think of relatives, friends, neighbors, people at church, school, or work who could use the gift of hope. Think of ways you can help bring hope to at least some of those on your list. Jot down everyone's suggestions next to the names on the list.

Here are a few ideas to help you get started:

Make a handmade card of encouragement for someone on your list. Have everyone in the family jot down a message. Then sign it and drop it in the mail the very same day!

Choose someone on the list that would appreciate a cheerful phone conversation, like an elderly aunt or uncle confined in bed. (For kids who are hesitant talkers, let them know that it's okay to say something as simple as: "Hi. I'm praying for you. And I'm sending a hug." Thoughtful words can brighten anyone's day!) So pick up the phone and give someone a call. Spread the message of hope!

Think of someone who lives alone or who's new to the area. Surprise them by caroling at their door!

Putting It into Practice...

Select a name (or several names) from the list and work to bring hope to them throughout the week or even throughout all of Advent!

To keep track of your family's progress use the "Heart Chart" pictured below. Every time someone offers hope to someone on the list, add a "Handful of Hope" to the chart. Each night, either before or after dinner, allow some time for reflecting on the day and for each person to add the appropriate number of handfuls of hope.

Heart Chart

Supplies needed:

poster board

construction paper

scissors

craft glue

Directions:

1. Cut a large heart from poster board.

2. Have each member of the family trace their hands on construction paper. Then have them cut out the handprints and print the word "HOPE" on each. Save these handprints for later.

3. Whenever a family member offers hope to someone on the list, that person should glue a "handful of Hope" to the heart chart.

Handfuls of Hope

Second Week of Advent

The main theme for the second week of Advent is "preparing" for Christ's coming; the secondary theme is peace.

Week Two provides plenty of crafts and gift-making ideas to help children prepare for the coming celebration of Christ's birth. Because we're also preparing their hearts for the coming Prince of Peace, this week contains peace-making activities.

As with all the weeks of Advent, please glance through each section ahead of time so you are familiar with the various activities. Some activities will require advance planning because you'll need to round up supplies. You may want to look ahead to the "Birthday Party for Jesus" (page 93), which comes after Week Four. If you choose to hold a party, you'll want to plan for that now. Also, make sure to flip to the back of the book where you will find reproducible puzzles and games.

May the peace of Jesus dwell in your hearts during Advent and every day of the year.

Week-at-a-Glance

A Hand-made C

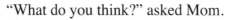

"What do you think?" asked Mom.

"Great!" said Theo.

"Yeah, great!" echoed Herbert.

"Cool!" Gabe and Mike said together in their weird twin way.

"Okay!" piped Joey, my youngest little brother.

Mom turned to me. "Sophie?"

I knew that Mom wanted me to like her idea about making our Christmas gifts for each other this year. But can you imagine what kind of presents my three- to six-year-old brothers might make for me? "I don't know," I said.

"Come on," said Mom. "A hand-made Christmas will be fun."

My little brothers all begged, "Come on, Sophie!"

"Okay, already!" I yelled over the noise.

"Yeah!" shouted Joey. "Yippee!" (He's way into cheering!)

Over the next week, the boys acted so-o-o secretive about the gifts they were making. They kept borrowing things from me like crayons and markers and other supplies. And they kept saying "mysterious" stuff like, "You'll never guess what I'm making, Sophie!" Like they could be making anything good with old tissue boxes and cardboard!

I tried to convince Mom that this hand-made Christmas was a bad idea.

"Who knows what they'll come up with?" I said.

"That's the fun of it!" said Mom.

I switched into whine mode. "Couldn't we just do things like we did when Dad was here?" Before their separation, either Mom or Dad took each of the boys shopping, adding to the money they'd saved and helping them pick out good gifts.

"We can't afford that," said Mom quietly.

I didn't want Mom to feel bad, so I quit complaining. But I still didn't want a hand-made Christmas!

On Christmas Eve, I made bookmarks for my brothers just before we went to Mass. Usually I was so happy about going to

The Advent–Christmas Book

ristmas

By Diana Jenkins
Illustrated by Mary Rojas

the special service and opening gifts afterward. This year Christmas was no big deal!

The Mass was lovely, but I just couldn't get into it. My brothers were all singing too loudly, Dad wasn't with us, and Mom looked sad. This had to be the worst Christmas Ever!

When we started opening our gifts back at home, the boys liked their bookmarks and Mom immediately put on the necklace I'd made her. I loved the nightgown she'd sewn for me!

Maybe this won't be so bad, I thought.

Then Joey handed me his hand-made gift. It was lump-shaped and heavy as a rock. When I got it open, I discovered that it was a rock that Joey had colored with crayons!

"Do you love it?" he asked.

"Uh, yeah," I said. "Thanks!"

Gabe and Mike handed me what looked like a wrapped-up tissue box.

I unwrapped it and found—"surprise!"—a tissue box that had been decorated within an inch of its life. Something rattled so I peered inside and saw two small white things. When I realized what they were, I went, "Ewwwww!"

"Sophie!" scolded Mom.

"I mean....Oooh what a great gift!" I forced a smile onto my face while my mind wondered why my brothers would give me teeth as a present!

Herbert pushed his gift into my hand. It looked like a scroll tied up with yarn. I took off the yarn and unrolled at least six feet of paper!

From one end to the other, it was filled with scribbles!

"I wrote it myself!" said Herbert.

"No kidding!" I said sarcastically. When Mom frowned at me, I added, "Thanks!"

I still had one little glimmer of hope that Theo might come up with a decent present! But, no, he gave me a piece of

cardboard with rainbows drawn on it and a penny glued to the middle! A penny!

"Gee, thanks, Theo," I said. "This is really too much!"

That night before I went to bed, I laid my brothers' stupid gifts out on my desk and just stared at them. What a bunch of junk! I thought, tossing it all in my wastebasket.

The next morning, the boys burst into my room like they always do on Christmas.

"Get up!" they shouted. I pulled the covers over my head and said, "Go away!"

"Get up!" cried Theo.

"We're having pancakes!" shouted Herbert.

"We're hungry!" yelled the twins.

"Hey, why is my rock in the trash?" said Joey.

Busted! I thought, burrowing further under the blankets.

I heard the boys rummaging in the wastebasket and saying things like "What's this doing in here?" I thought about sneaking out then, but suddenly things got quiet. I knew that every eye was turned my way!

I finally got up the nerve to peep out. "Sorry! I guess they accidentally fell off my desk...or something."

"Oh, okay!" said Joey, stroking his rock like it was a kitten.

"Don't you just love it?"

"I sure do!" I said.

"It's a creek rock," he said.

"It sure...." That's when I remembered the day that Joey and I walked to the creek. We had had such a fun time that Joey wanted to bring back a big rock.

This big rock!

That rock meant so much to Joey! And he was giving it to me!

"You forgot to put the teeth under your pillow!" said the twins.

Oh, yeah, I thought. Whenever the twins lose teeth, they put them under their pillow and make a wish. And they were giving their wishes to me!

After I promised to do the tooth thing that night, I asked Herbert what his scroll said. He "read" me something like, "Sophie is my sister and she is the best sister in the world and she reads to me because she is the best sister in the world and...." Well, you get the idea!

"Theo," I said after that, "is there something special about that penny?"

"Sure!" he said, handing me the card. "It's Dad's lucky penny that he gave to me before he left."

I don't believe in lucky pennies, but right then I felt like the luckiest big sister in the world! I'd given my brothers last-minute, slap-dash presents, and they had given me gifts that really meant something! Gifts they made in their hearts before they made them with their hands.

"Thanks, you guys!" I jumped up and hugged each brother. "These are the best presents ever!"

"Yay!" cheered Joey. I laughed and said, "You don't need to cheer for me!" Like I deserved that! "I'm not," he said, sniffing the air. "I'm cheering for the pancakes!" We all hurrahed then and hurried down to breakfast. I couldn't wait to tell Mom how much I loved our hand-made Christmas! Maybe, I thought, we should call it "heart-made!"

Advent Wreath Ceremony

The Advent wreath symbolizes our time of waiting, our time of hoping. It helps us mark our days until Christmas.

This Advent wreath ceremony provides you with an opportunity to pass on tradition, to share Scripture and prayer, and to help children understand that Christ is at the center of our days of waiting.

The ceremony takes only minutes, making it easy to incorporate into busy days. One person reads the Scripture passage, another reads the prayer, another lights the candle, then everyone joins in with the response. (Do not leave burning candles unattended.)

Isaiah 11:10

The time is coming when one of David's descendants will be the signal for the people of all nations to come together. They will follow his advice, and his own nation will become famous.

Reader:

Dear Lord,
as we light this second candle,
we wait anxiously
for Christmas to come.
We pray that one day soon
all nations will stand united,
all people will live in peace,
and that all people
will come to know you
and claim you
as Prince of Peace.
Amen.

Light two purple candles.

All:

Come, Jesus, Prince of Peace.
Come, Lord Jesus, come.

Psalm 85:8, 10-11

I will listen to you, Lord God,
because you promise peace
to those who are faithful
and no longer foolish.
Love and loyalty
will come together;
goodness and peace
will unite.
Loyalty will sprout
from the ground;
justice will look down
from the sky above.

Reader:

> Dear Jesus,
> during these days of Advent,
> let us work for peace in our hearts
> and in our homes,
> let us work for peace in our schools
> and in our places of work,
> in our communities
> and in the entire world.
> Amen.

> > *Light two purple candles.*

All:

> Come, Jesus, Prince of Peace.
> Come, Lord Jesus, come.

Week 2
TUE

Mark 1:1-3

This is the good news about Jesus Christ, the Son of God. It began just as God had said in the book written by Isaiah the prophet, "I am sending my messenger to get the way ready for you. In the desert someone is shouting, 'Get the road ready for the Lord! Make a straight path for him.'"

Reader:

> Heavenly Father,
> you sent John the Baptist
> to prepare the way for Jesus.
> As John led others to Jesus,
> help me to lead others to Jesus, too.
> Help me to teach others about Jesus
> by the things that I say and do.
> Amen.

> > *Light two purple candles.*

All:

> Come, Jesus, Prince of Peace.
> Come, Lord Jesus, come.

Week 2
WED

Mark 1:4, 7-8

So John the Baptist showed up in the desert and told everyone, "Turn back to God and be baptized! Then your sins will be forgiven." John also told the people, "Someone more powerful is going to come. And I am not good enough even to stoop down and untie his sandals. I baptize you with water, but he will baptize you with the Holy Spirit!"

Reader:

> Lord God, thank you
> for the gift of John the Baptist.
> Thank you for the gift of Baptism.
> Thank you for the gift
> of your Holy Spirit.
> Thank you for the gift
> of your Son. Amen.

> > *Light two purple candles.*

All:

> Come, Jesus, Prince of Peace.
> Come, Lord Jesus, come.

Week 2
THU

2 Peter 3:10, 14

The day of the Lord's return will surprise us like a thief. My friends, while you are waiting, you should make certain that the Lord finds you pure, spotless and living at peace.

Reader:

Sweet Jesus,
as we wait anxiously
for your second coming,
we live in faith
by spreading your message
of hope, peace, and love.
Amen.

Light two purple candles.

All:

Come, Jesus, Prince of Peace.
Come, Lord Jesus, come.

Week 2
FRI

Isaiah 60:4-6

The Lord said: Open your eyes! Look around! Crowds are coming. Your sons are on their way from distant lands; your daughters are being carried like little children. When you see this, your faces will glow; your hearts will pound and swell with pride…. Your country will be covered with caravans of young camels…. The people of Sheba will bring gold and spices in praise of me, the Lord.

Reader:

Lord God,
people of old praised you,
by giving you gifts of spices and gold.
We, too, praise you,
with gifts from our hearts—
kind deeds and peaceful words.
Amen.

Light two purple candles.

All:

Come, Jesus, Prince of Peace.
Come, Lord Jesus, come.

Week 2
SAT

Romans 15:4-5

And the Scriptures were written to teach and encourage us by giving us hope. God is the one who makes us patient and cheerful. I pray that he will help you live at peace with each other, as you follow Christ.

Reader:

Dear Jesus,
you are the perfect Teacher.
You show us the perfect path.
Please help us follow in your footsteps
by bringing your love,
your joy, and your peace
into your world.
Amen.

Light two purple candles.

All:

Come, Jesus, Prince of Peace.
Come, Lord Jesus, come.

I-Give-My-Heart-to-Jesus Ornament

Easy

This is a great project for kids with little hands and big hearts!

Supplies needed:

craft foam sheet

OR clean Styrofoam™ tray (the type used in produce departments at grocery stores)

heart-shaped cookie cutter or heart template made from cardboard

permanent marker

scissors

hole punch

clear-drying craft glue

photo of child

beads, sequins, glitter

ribbon

Directions:

1. Press heart-shaped cookie cutter into foam sheet or Styrofoam™ tray to make outline of heart. If you are using the cardboard heart template, trace template onto foam sheet or Styrofoam™ with permanent marker.

2. Cut along outline of heart.

3. Use hole punch to punch hole near top of ornament.

4. Thread ribbon through hole. Tie ends to form loop for hanging.

5. With permanent marker write: "I give my heart to Jesus" on back of heart. Write date on ornament, too.

6. Glue photo onto front of the heart.

7. Decorate front of ornament by gluing glitter, sequins, and/or beads onto ornament. Set aside to dry.

front

back

Reflection

The holidays demand an immese outpouring of energy from any parent planning and baking and buying in order to bring family members the fullness of Christmas joys. Yet simultaneously with the holiday preparations, we are plunged into the darkness, emptiness and longing of Advent. The haunting strains of "O come, O come, Emmanuel," echo in our hearts as we scramble for some time to attune our souls to the melody of Advent waiting. In the time we can snatch between errands and appointments to "tune in" to God, we beg him to invade our own lives.

Sr. Kathryn James Hermes, FSP

Tin-Punch Ornaments

These tin-punch ornaments hold symbols of the season. You can choose symbols from the list below or design a few of your own.

Star Reminds us of Jesus, the Light of the World or the Bethlehem star that led the wise men to Jesus.

Cross Reminds us of Jesus, our Savior and Lord.

Crown Reminds us of Jesus, the King of kings.

Cane Reminds us of Jesus, the Good Shepherd.

Manger Reminds us of Jesus' humble birth.

Heart Reminds us of God's love.

Supplies needed:

tin lids from frozen juice cans (one for each ornament to be made)

permanent marker

hammers

nails, different gauges

clear-drying craft glue

glitter

paper

pencils

piece of wood bigger than lid for each child

strand of mini beads (optional)

string, ribbon, or cording

Directions:

1. Wash and dry tin lids from cans of frozen juice.

2. Children can practice drawing the symbol they wish to use with paper and pencil (see diagrams). Then draw symbols on the lid with permanent marker.

3. Place lid on wood and then, using a hammer and a variety of nails, punch holes into lid. (Ornaments look best when holes vary in size.)

4. Squeeze clear-drying craft glue around rim of lid, then dip lid into glitter. Let dry.

5. (Optional) Glue strand of beads near lip of lid, next to glitter.

6. When the ornament is dry, use a larger nail to punch a wide hole near top of lid. Thread string, ribbon, or cording through hole and tie to form loop for hanging.

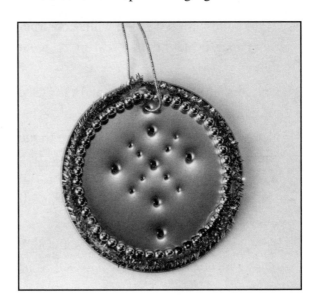

Dove Ornament

The dove is a symbol of peace and a symbol of the Holy Spirit.

Supplies needed:

Two 5" x 9" pieces of white tissue paper

5" x 4" piece of white construction paper, poster board or foam sheet

3" x 3" piece of red construction paper or foam sheet

1" x 1" piece of green construction paper or fabric

6" of ribbon or cording

2 tiny beads for eyes

clear-drying craft glue

cellophane tape   ruler

pointed scissors   pencil

large-eyed embroidery needle

Directions:

1. Photocopy template on this page and cut them out.

2. Trace pattern for dove onto white construction paper, poster board, or foam, then cut out.

3. Cut slits in body for wings and tail. (See template.)

4. Cut two 5 by 9 inch pieces of white tissue paper. Fold each accordion-style, starting with short end, fold up 1/2 inch then flip paper over and repeat until paper is all folded.

5. Trim corners, then slide "wings" through middle slit and "tail" through other slit. Tape "tail" together at center to form a semi-circle.

6. Trace heart from template onto red construction paper or foam sheet.

7. Glue beads in place for eyes, and heart on dove's chest.

8. Trace and cut out leaf from green construction paper or fabric

9. Cut 1/4 inch slit in beak. Slide leaf into place and glue.

10. Use embroidery needle to pull ribbon (or cording) through body. Tie ends together to form loop for hanging.

Helping Hands Ornament

Easy

This ornament contains an extra gift: the scroll. Written inside the scroll is a secret "good deed." The child commits himself or herself to doing the "good deed" during Advent. The child can promise to say an extra prayer for world peace, do the dishes, or bring hope to someone by visiting or calling an elderly relative.

Supplies needed:

craft foam sheets or construction paper

pen

scissors

ruler

hole punch

ribbon

clear-drying craft glue

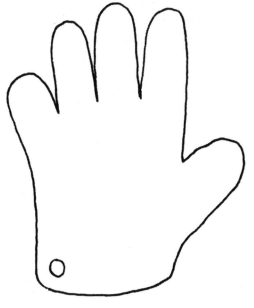

Directions:

1. Photocopy template on this page and cut it out. Trace pattern onto foam sheet or construction paper. Or you may want to have child trace his or her hand onto foam sheet.

2. Cut "hand print" from foam.

3. Using hole punch, make a hole near "wrist" opposite thumb.

4. Thread ribbon through hole. Tie ends to form loop for hanging.

5. Cut a rectangle measuring 1 1/2 by 1 3/4 inches from a different color of foam or construction paper.

6. Brainstorm ideas for good deeds. Have each child write his/her secret "good deed" on the rectangle, then roll up the rectangle to form a scroll and tie it closed with the ribbon.

7. Glue scroll to "hand print."

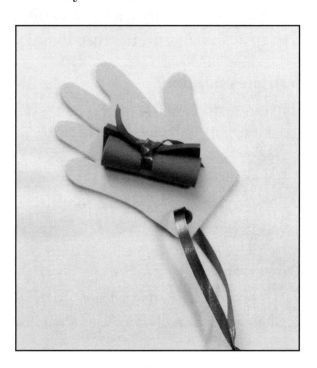

Sweet-Scented, Glittery-Gold Pine Cone Ornament

The three wise men brought the newborn King of kings three special gifts: gold, frankincense, and myrrh. The gold was in honor of the kingly status of Jesus. The frankincense foreshadowed the infant's role as priest. And the gift of myrrh reminds us of Jesus' passion and death and our salvation. These sweet-scented, glittery gold ornaments will help remind children of the first gifts presented to Jesus and their symbolism.

Supplies needed:

pine cones (at least one per child)

clear-drying craft glue

cinnamon or pumpkin pie spice

gold glitter

ribbon, yarn, or gold elastic cording

wax paper

Directions:

1. Gather pine cones from outdoors.

2. Tap pine cones gently to loosen dirt and dust from tips.

3. Cut a 10 inch piece of ribbon, yarn, or elastic cording. Tie ribbon, yarn, or cording tightly around top of pinecone, securing with a double knot. To form loop for hanging, tie ends with another double knot.

4. Dab inside the tips of the pine cone with glue, then sprinkle spice onto the glue. Place pine cone on wax paper to dry.

5. Once glue has dried, dab the tips of the pine cone with craft glue. Sprinkle gold glitter over glue. Place on wax paper to dry.

6. Keep as an ornament for your tree, or give as a gift. If the children want to give this ornament as a gift, they can include a note to explain the significance of the ornament.

Reflection

"Against the background of the serious situation of today's 'wilderness' the believer must, like John the Baptist, become a voice that proclaims the Lord's salvation by fully adhering to his Gospel and witnessing to it visibly in the world."

John Paul II

My Little Light Ornament

Easy

These ornaments clip right onto the branches of a Christmas tree!

Supplies needed:

   flat, pinch-style clothespins
   yellow, green, red, and white foam
      sheets
   sequins
   scissors
   hole punch
   clear-drying craft glue
   pencils

Directions:

1. Make a copy of the templates on this page and cut them out.

2. Trace the leaf template onto green foam sheet. Each child needs 3 leaves. Cut out leaves.

3. Trace the flame template onto the yellow foam sheet and the candle template onto the white foam sheet. (Note: Any color can be used for the candle.) Cut them out.

4. Use the hole punch to make "berries" from the red foam sheet.

5. Glue the "candle" onto the clothespin, then glue flame, holly leaves and berries onto clothespin.

6. Glue sequins onto flame. Let the ornament dry completely before using.

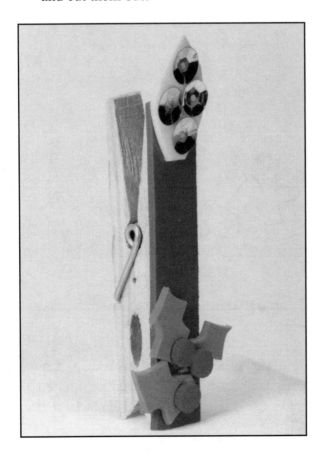

Art Projects and Field Trips

Family craft-time can be a time of great fun. It can provide busy families with a special opportunity for shared conversations and lots of laughter, plus sweet memories for down the road! So why not gather your family together and spend an evening crafting homemade ornaments for family and friends! Who knows…it may become one of your family's treasured traditions.

For you "craftsy" teachers out there, ornaments can make wonderful art projects, too. Your students can make a variety of ornaments to be given as gifts to family and friends. If you plan ahead, you can combine a service project with this art project, too! Simply have each of your students craft a handful of ornaments. Then plan a field trip to a nearby nursing home where students can present the residents with their ornaments as gifts, along with handwritten letters or cards. For an extra treat, you and your students can supply cookies (check first with the nursing home) and caroling, too!

Consider making an ornament for someone special on this list or invite the children to brainstorm names of people who could use a simple, handmade gift from the heart.

Mom	Cousins	Office ladies at school
Dad	Friends	Playground monitors
Brothers	Teachers	Mail Carrier
Sisters	Principal	Coaches
Grandmas	School nurse	Elderly neighbors
Grandpas	Custodians at school	Nursing home residents
Aunts	Crossing guards	Patients in hospitals
Uncles	Cafeteria workers	Prisoners

Helping Hand Coupons

Easy

These coupons make great gifts. We prepare for the coming of Jesus by growing in love for others and by working for peace. Photocopy the coupons on page 47 and 48 for each child (the pages need to be backed up). Coupons can be used during Advent or inserted into a Christmas card given and placed under the tree.

Helping Hand Coupons

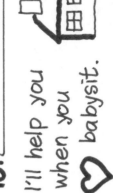

TO: _____

I'll help you clean your room.

TO: _____

I'll help you when you babysit.

I'll make your favorite snack for you.

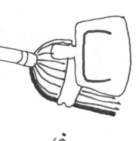

TO: _____

I'll watch your favorite video with you.

TO: _____

I'll help you with a school project.

TO: _____

I'll play your favorite game with you.

I'll sing you a song.

TO: _____

I'll do one of your chores.

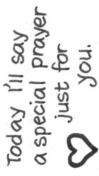

TO: _____

Today I'll say a special prayer just for you.

TO: _____

I'll take a walk with you.

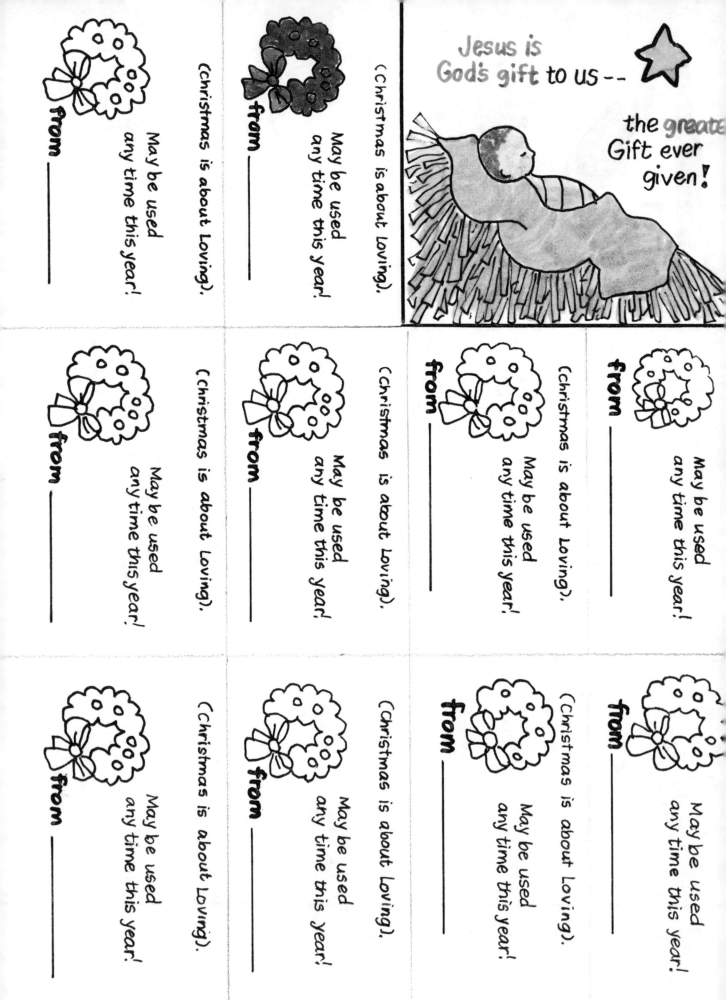

Angelic Memo Holders

In the story of Jesus' birth, the archangel Gabriel tells Mary of God's wonderful plan. Mary is then able to prepare for the coming of Jesus. Angels also sing of "peace on earth" the night of Jesus' birth in the manger. These memo holders are a reminder of the angels' message of peace as we prepare for the coming of Christ.

Supplies needed:

white poster paper or thick white paper

pencils

scissors

paints, crayons, or markers

glitter

white glue

craft glue

wooden clothespins (the kind that you pinch to open and close)

strip of magnet (can be purchased at most craft stores)

Directions:

1. Using poster paper or thick white paper have children draw an angel freehand. Option: make template and have children trace onto paper.

2. Children can color angel using paints, crayons, or markers. At the bottom of the angel's garment, the children can write "PEACE!"

3. Using white glue, children can add glitter wherever they wish.

4. Cut out the angel once the glitter has dried.

5. Attach a strip of magnet to one flat side of the clothespin.

6. Using craft glue, glue the other flat side of clothespin to the angel. Let it dry for about 25 minutes.

OPTIONAL:

On a separate piece of paper, children can write a prayer or message for the recipient of their gift. Clip the note in the clothespin.

Cinn-a-minn-ie Ornaments

These cinnamon scented ornaments are a snap to make! Use cookie cutters in the shape of stars, crowns, hearts, sheep, or shepherds' staffs to make sweet smelling symbols of the season to hang on a Christmas tree!

Please note that although these ornaments are made of applesauce and cinnamon, they are not edible.

Supplies needed:

3/4 cup applesauce

3/4 cup cinnamon

medium-sized mixing bowl

rolling pin

cookie cutters

toothpicks

wire cookie rack for drying ornaments

ribbon

Directions:

1. Measure applesauce into bowl and then add cinnamon a little bit at a time while mixing. The dough will be stiff when all the cinnamon is incorporated.

2. Sprinkle cinnamon on the counter. Turn dough out onto counter and knead dough by hand for a few minutes to make sure cinnamon and applesauce are well mixed.

3. Sprinkle more cinnamon on counter, then roll dough until it is about a 1/4 inch thick.

4. Use various cookie cutters to cut shapes from dough. Make sure the shapes represent symbols of the season.

5. Using a toothpick, form a hole at the top of the ornament large enough to thread ribbon through.

6. Place ornaments on wire cookie rack to dry for 2 days. After the first day, carefully turn ornaments over to help them dry completely.

7. After the ornaments are completely dry, thread ribbon through the hole. Tie ends together to form a loop for hanging the ornament.

Reflection

O Daystar of unending light,
the sun of God's pure holiness,
the splendor of the Father's face,
and image of his graciousness.
O come! O come!
And lead us forth from darkness
and the gloom of death.

O Antiphon for December 21

Not-to-Eat Dough Ornaments

These dough ornaments look good enough to eat–but they're not. They're made with glue!

Supplies needed:

1/2 cup flour

1/2 cup cornstarch

1/2 cup white craft glue

medium sized bowl

food coloring

paint brush

fine-tip permanent markers

toothpick

ribbon

wire cookie rack

optional: rolling pin and cookie cutters

Directions:

1. Before mixing the dough, have children brainstorm for possible seasonal shapes they want their ornaments to have.

2. Measure and mix flour and cornstarch in medium sized bowl.

3. Add glue. Mix well.

4. Remove dough from bowl and place on counter. Knead dough by hand until it is smooth. Since this dough isn't sticky, there's no need to add flour to the counter.

5. Have children form dough into desired shapes, or they can roll dough with rolling pin until dough is a 1/4 inch thick. Cut out shapes with cookie cutters.

6. With toothpick, make a hole near the top of the ornament. The hole needs to be large enough to thread ribbon through once the ornament dries.

7. Let ornaments dry for 2 days on wire cookie rack. Turn ornaments over every 12 hours so they dry evenly.

8. When ornaments are completely dry, mix a small amount of glue and food coloring to make "paint" for the ornaments.

9. Paint ornaments, then place them again on the wire cookie rack to dry.

10. Fine details can be added with permanent markers after the paint has completely dried.

11. Thread ribbon through the hole. Tie ends together to form a loop for hanging the ornament.

Traditions create memories. Memories enrich our lives. Traditions help us pass on valuable lessons to our children and our children's children.

Making and/or Giving Ornaments

Some families are blessed with an "artsy" aunt or talented grandpa who enjoys crafting beautiful, personalized ornaments for family and friends—year after year after year.

When these treasured keepsakes perennially grace Christmas trees, they evoke memories of Christmases past, of loved ones long gone, and they become symbols of love.

For those of you who aren't terribly good with arts or crafts, here are a few customs you might want to consider.…

At the beginning of each Advent season, purchase an annual "keepsake" ornament—not a whimsical one, but one that serves as a symbol of the season. Get your children involved, too. Enlist their help in selecting your family's annual symbolic ornament. (If the ornament isn't dated, you can date it later with a permanent marker.)

Let these annual, symbolic "keepsakes" grace your tree as visual reminders that Jesus is at the center of your waiting and your celebrations.

Another beautiful tradition is for each child to have his or her own special "Christmas Keepsake Box." This box should be large enough to hold two dozen or more ornaments. It isn't necessary to purchase a special box. Adult-sized shoe boxes that contained boots are often big enough. Simply decorate the outside of the box with contact paper, wrapping paper, and/or stickers. Make sure that each box is clearly marked with your child's name.

Starting with your baby's first Christmas (or whenever you decide to begin this family tradition), an ornament is selected, dated, and hung on your tree, then stored away in that child's "Christmas Keepsake Box" until the following Advent season. Each year an ornament is given to each child, preferably one with a spiritual meaning. Make sure to take time with your child to discuss the spiritual meaning of the ornament you have chosen.

Each year the collection grows. By the time the children are adults and have moved out on their own, they'll have their own treasure boxes full of meaningful memories to hang on their trees. And thus, the tradition continues.…

Second Week of Advent

Take-home pages offer a variety of activities that support what we're learning at school. We'd like you to consider choosing a few of these activities that you can share with your child and family at home.

Take one or two nights this week to share with your family the anticipation of the Advent season. Plan early in the week the evenings you will come together to participate in these activities.

Some of the activities call for quiet reflection; some require an activity or project. Please read over the entire handout to see if advance planning is needed for any of the activities you choose to do.

During the first week of Advent we focused on bringing hope into the world. During the second week of Advent we focus on preparing our hearts for the coming of the Prince of Peace. We prepare by growing in holiness; we prepare by working for peace; we prepare by growing in love.

The following activities are designed to help your family become more aware that peace begins within each of us, is shared within our families, and then carried into the world.

Warm-Up Exercises

1. Together with your family, deliberately and in a reflective manner pray the Prayer of St. Francis of Assisi.

> Lord, make me an instrument of your peace.
> Where there is hatred, let me sow love.
> Where there is injury, pardon.
> Where there is doubt, faith.
> Where there is despair, hope.
> Where there is darkness, light.
> Where there is sadness, joy.
> O Divine Master, grant that I may not so much seek to be consoled, as to console;
> to be understood, as to understand;
> To be loved, as to love;
> For it is in giving that we receive;
> It is in pardoning, that we are pardoned;
> and it is in dying, that we are born to eternal life.

Discuss what each line means. Refrain from supplying an answer when there are moments of silence. Allow God to work in the silence so that the answers come from all the members of your family and not just one or two people. (You might want to post this prayer in a place where your children will see it on a daily basis: perhaps on the refrigerator, the bathroom mirror, or the front.)

Next, ask your family to brainstorm names of well-known peacemakers. Why are they considered to be peacemakers? What did they do? What didn't they do? Ask your children to describe a peacemaker. Ask if they can think of family members or friends who are peacemakers? Challenge each member of your family to think what makes them peacemakers?

Now brainstorm with your family the ways that each of you can be peacemakers at home. Then have everyone choose one way that they plan to bring peace to your family this Advent.

Getting Started...

2. Gather around the Advent wreath. Light two purple candles and read the following passage from Scripture. If this activity is be-

ing done on a separate night from the Warm-Up Exercises before reading the Gospel, begin by praying the Prayer of St. Francis together.

You know that our ancestors were told, "Do not murder" and "A murderer must be brought to trial." But I promise you that if you are angry with someone, you will stand trial.... So if you are about to place your gift on the altar and remember that someone is angry with you, leave your gift there in front of the altar. Make peace with that person, then come back and offer your gift to God" (Mt 5:21–24).

Now ask everyone to think about someone who has hurt them, someone they need to forgive. Then encourage everyone to pray in silence for those individuals.

Here comes the hard part...encourage everyone in your family to make amends with the person who has offended them before the day is over. Explain to them that the means of communication doesn't matter, but forgiveness and reconciliation do. Tell them they can offer forgiveness in person, they can call by phone, they can write a letter, or send an e-mail message. What is important is the peace that comes from forgiveness and reconciliation.

Reconcile with God.

Reconcile with others.

Help bring peace to a hurting world.

Putting It into Practice...

3. It's time to conduct some research—family style! The first resource will be the Bible. The second will involve the Internet. If you don't have Internet access at home, plan a family field trip to your local library. It will be well worth your time!

First, check out the following verses from the Bible:

Romans 14:19

Proverbs 14:29

Proverbs 15:1

Proverbs 15:18

Proverbs 16:24

Proverbs 17:14

Proverbs 19:17.

Have each member of the family look up a different verse and then share it with each other.

Discuss how these verses relate to peace.

Second, find out how others work for peace. For starters, visit the websites of these organizations.

Peace Through Love—Kids for Peace

Kids Care Story Center

PlanetPals (planetpals.com)

Catholic Relief Services (catholicrelief.org)

United National Cyberschoolbus

Free the Children (freethechildren.org)

Peace Games (peacegames.org)

After exploring these websites, discuss why it's important to be united with others in our work for peace.

Choose a peace project your family can work on together (and with others) to help bring peace to our world. Don't wait for tomorrow, jump right in today!

Reflection

"Yesterday is gone.
Tomorrow has not yet come.
We have only today.
Let us begin."

Mother Teresa

Third Week of Advent

The main theme for the third week of Advent is joy; the secondary theme is light. We rejoice that Advent is half over and Christmas is almost here. We also joyfully carry Christ's light into the world.

Week Three provides plenty of crafts and gift-making ideas to help you prepare for the coming celebration of Christ's birth.

It also suggests activities for making this world a better place, activities that help to illuminate the world by sharing the light of Christ.

As with all weeks of Advent, please glance through each section so you are familiar with the week's various activities. Some will require advance planning because you'll need to round up supplies. If you're planning on holding a "Birthday Party for Jesus," you'll want to take care of some of those details now. See the "Birthday Party" section that follows Week Four (page 93). Please make sure to flip to the back of the book to find reproducible puzzles and games.

Week-at-a-Glance

Christmas Reflections

By Christine
Virginia Orfeo, FSP
Illustrated by
Steve Delmonte

"I can't believe Mrs. Stowe gave us homework over Christmas break," muttered Doug.

He pushed his notebook aside with a sigh. He looked longingly out his bedroom window where the snow was falling silently. He could see down the road that joined his home to the Shrine of Our Lady. Tomorrow, carloads of visitors would arrive to admire the Christmas Festival display. Doug's parents worked at the shrine and were responsible for the organization of the festival that took place before Christmas each year.

"Doug, are you finished with your homework yet?" Mom called from downstairs. "We have a lot of signs to put up, and your father still has to set up some of the outside Christmas scenes."

"I can help, Mom," said Doug, as he came downstairs with his coat. "I can't think of what to write my paper about anyway."

"What paper is that?" asked his Mom.

"Oh, Mrs. Stowe wants us to write about what lessons we can learn from Christmas. I don't even know what she means." Doug pulled on his boots. "I mean, Christmas is a time to enjoy celebrating. Why drag school stuff into it?"

"Hmmm," said his mother absently, wrapping

her scarf around her neck. "Maybe you'll get some inspiration tonight."

That night, before the festival opened, Doug and his parents, and the other staff of the shrine (including Doug's friend, Sister Margaret) would have a sneak preview of the international nativity display. There were crèches from all over the world. They had figures of Mary, Joseph, Jesus, shepherds, and wise men made out of every type of material imaginable. Some were hand-carved wood, others were bamboo, clay, stone, or fabric. They ranged from life-sized down to tiny miniatures.

Doug and his parents had finished the rest of the setting up by the time it was dark. After a quick supper, they hurried over to tour all the nativity sets. Doug loved looking at all of them. But there was one special set he'd have to wait to see.

"No, you can't see it either," Sister Margaret had said with a smile. "You're no exception to the rule. I want to keep mine a surprise."

"But tomorrow I'll be helping to welcome the visitors at the information table. I won't have time to see it," pleaded Doug.

"No," said Sister Margaret, laughing. "I think you'll be able to find a few minutes to sneak over to see it!"

But the next day, Doug was kept very busy until late afternoon. Sister Margaret came through the crowds looking for him.

"Doug, have you seen it yet?" she asked. She looked so excited that Doug became even more curious than ever.

What could be so special about this nativity scene?

"Not yet, Sister," said Doug. "But I really want to."

"I'll stay here at the table so you you can go," she said.

"It must be a really cool nativity set. You seem so excited about it!" said Doug with a grin.

Sister Margaret threw back her head and laughed. "Christmas always makes me feel excited—like a kid on Christmas morning! Go on now. I want to know what you think of my nativity set."

Doug made his way through all the people filling the shrine. When he got to the chapel where the mystery nativity was, there was a huge line. The "Ooooos" and "Ahhhs" coming from the front of the line made waiting

"Doug, have you seen it yet?"
Sr. Margaret asked.
She looked so excited that
Doug became even more
curious than ever.
What could be so special
about this nativity scene?

unbearable. Was the thing made of solid gold or what?!

Finally it was Doug's turn. He had noticed people bending down to peer inside a box. Now he looked into the square opening. The familiar figures of Mary and Joseph knelt next to Jesus, lying in the manger. The donkey and the cow reclined on the straw. The shepherds and wise men were there, too. The figures were all made of smooth, clear glass. But suddenly, Doug realized that the inside of the stable was all mirrors. When he looked at each character in just the right way, the set-up of the mirrors showed him his own face on the face of the figure.

He leaned a little to the side, and there he was as a shepherd!

He leaned a little the other way, and there he was as Joseph!

For a moment, it seemed that time stood still.

Imagine, he thought. To have been right there, in the stable, when Jesus was born….

Doug came back to earth as he heard the people behind him in line getting impatient. He got up and went to find Sister Margaret. He just had to talk to her about this amazing nativity. He knew now he would have no problem writing his paper for Mrs. Stowe.

Reprinted from *My Friend—A Catholic Magazine for Kids*, Pauline Books & Media, 50 Saint Pauls Avenue, Boston, MA 02130. www.myfriendmagazine.com

The Advent–Christmas Book

Advent Wreath Ceremony

The Advent wreath symbolizes our time of waiting, our time of hoping. It helps us mark our days until Christmas.

This Advent wreath ceremony provides teachers and parents with an opportunity to pass on tradition, to share Scripture and prayer, and to help children understand that Christ is at the center of our days of waiting.

The ceremony takes only minutes, making it easy to incorporate into busy days. One person reads the Scripture passage, another reads the prayer, another lights the candle, then everyone joins in with the response. (Do not leave burning candles unattended.)

John 1:6–9

God sent a man named John, who came to tell about the light and to lead all people to have faith. John wasn't that light. He came only to tell about the light. The true light that shines on everyone was coming into the world.

Reader:

> Heavenly Father,
> we're half way through Advent.
> Two weeks have already passed.
> As we light this pink Advent candle,
> we think of Jesus,
> the Light of the World.
> May we, as followers of Jesus,
> carry the light of your love
> into the world.
> Amen.

Light the pink candle and two purple candles.

All:

> Come, Jesus, Light of the World.
> Come, Lord Jesus, come.

Philippians 4:4–5

Always be glad because of the Lord! I will say it again: Be glad. Always be gentle with others. The Lord will soon be here.

Reader: (Poem)

> I'm trying hard
> to be like Jesus.
> I'm trying to be gentle,
> loving and kind.
> When I reach out
> to others in compassion,
> I know that my love
> for Jesus shines.

Light the pink candle and two purple candles.

All:

Come, Jesus, Light of the World.
Come, Lord Jesus, come.

Luke 1:46–47, 49

Mary said: "With all my heart I praise the Lord, and I am glad because of God, my Savior. God the All-Powerful has done great things for me, and his name is holy."

Reader:

Dear God,
may we, like Mary,
rejoice in your word
and accept your will
as we wait
for Jesus to come.
Amen.

Light the pink candle and two purple candles.

All:

Come, Jesus, Light of the World.
Come, Lord Jesus, come.

Isaiah 61:11

The LORD will bring about justice and praise in every nation on earth, like flowers blooming in a garden.

Reader:

Dear Lord,
we praise and honor you
by working for peace
and justice
today and always
until you come again.
Please help us in our efforts.
Amen.

Light the pink candle and two purple candles.

All:

Come, Jesus, Light of the World.
Come, Lord Jesus, come.

1 Thessalonians 5:16–18

Always be joyful and never stop praying. Whatever happens, keep thanking God because of Jesus Christ. This is what God wants you to do.

Reader:

Lord Jesus,
we praise you
and thank you always!
You are awesome,
O Lord, our God!
Amen.

Light the pink candle and two purple candles.

All:

Come, Jesus, Light of the World.
Come, Lord Jesus, come.

Week 3
FRI

James 5:7–8

My friends, be patient until the Lord returns. Think of farmers who wait patiently for the spring and summer rains to make their valuable crops grow. Be patient like those farmers and don't give up. The Lord will soon be here!

Reader:

Sweet Jesus,
as we wait patiently for your coming,
help us to let our lights shine
so the world will be aglow
with your love.
Amen.

Light the pink candle and two purple candles.

All:

Come, Jesus, Light of the World.
Come, Lord Jesus, come.

Week 3
SAT

Isaiah 9:2

Those who walked in the dark have seen a bright light. And it shines upon everyone who lives in the land of darkest shadows.

Reader:

Dear Jesus,
during this Advent season,
and throughout the days of our lives,
help us always
to share the light of your love

with our families and friends
and everyone we meet!
Amen.

Light the pink candle and two purple candles.

All:

Come, Jesus, Light of the World.
Come, Lord Jesus, come.

Reflection

Advent secrets for survival:

SET your alarm to wake you up ten minutes earlier than usual. Enjoy a quiet cup of coffee and talk to Jesus about your coming day.

MAKE a to-do list at night for the following day. Plan to do a reasonable amount of tasks, and when you're finished, take a walk, play with the kids, or make something creative to surprise someone.

WRITE your Christmas cards (except for those of your immediate family) by Thanksgiving. It'll make the holiday rush that much lighter.

PLAN five minutes of exercise into your day. Physical health is key to looking at life creatively and dynamically.

TAKE your family to see the sights and sounds of Christmas, and discover the holidays and holy days again through the eyes of a child.

Sr. Kathryn James Hermes, FSP

Magnets

Easy

These fun-to-make foam magnets are great note holders. The shapes remind us of attitudes and deeds that bring light to the world.

Supplies needed:

foam sheets (available in most craft
  and fabric stores)

flat, pinch-style clothespins

magnetic tape

craft glue

note cards

permanent markers (various colors)

Directions:

1. Photocopy templates on pages 63–64. Cut out templates.

2. Trace patterns onto foam sheets. Cut shapes from foam sheets and add details with markers.

3. Glue foam shapes onto clothespins. (The top of your shape should be at the open end of the clothespin.)

4. Cut a piece of magnetic tape long enough to fit clothespin. Press sticky side of magnetic tape to back of clothespin.

5. On a blank note card write a special message, then clip magnet to the card.

From the bottom of my heart! From the bottom of my heart! THANKS

Third Week of Advent

The Advent–Christmas Book

Stained Glass Window

This mini stained glass window can be hung on a window.

Supplies needed:

black poster board

newspaper

white typing or copy paper (Do not use construction paper. It's too thick.)

markers

black crayon

scissors

glue

cooking oil in small bowl

cotton ball

paper towel

hole punch

ribbon

Directions:

1. Cover work area with newspaper. On an 8 by 10 inch piece of black poster board draw and cut out a frame for stained glass window. The frame can be any shape desired but should be 2 inches in width all around.

2. To form "window" trace outline of "frame" onto white paper. Add 1 inch all around window and cut out.

3. Draw and color "window" design with markers. Design can be anything related to Advent, so be creative! The design should fit entirely in the window. It should not extend on the extra 1 inch around the design.

4. With black crayon, outline design. Then add lines to background to make it look like sec-tions of "stained glass." Make sure lines are thick and solid.

5. Turn "window" over. Dip cotton ball into cooking oil and rub gently over entire de-sign. Do not put oil on the extra 1 inch bor-der around the design. The oil will make the paper look transparent like glass. Use paper towel to gently wipe off excess oil.

6. Glue "frame" onto "window" by putting glue on the extra un-oiled 1 inch margin of the design.

7. Use the hole punch to punch a hole in top part of the "window frame."

8. Thread ribbon through hole. Tie ends to form loop. Hang in window.

Holy Family Keepsake

Notice the heart that embraces the "holy family" in this keepsake.

Supplies needed:

foam sheets (available to most craft and fabric stores)

fine-tip markers

white craft glue

a few pieces of straw

scissors

hole punch

ribbon

gift wrap tissue paper

pencil

Directions:

1. Trace template patterns onto foam sheets.
2. Cut stable from foam sheet. Using fine-tip marker, draw lines to resemble boards of wood.
3. Cut large heart from foam sheet. Glue onto stable.
4. Cut face from foam sheet. Glue faces onto large heart.
5. Cut "swaddling clothes" from foam sheet. Glue face onto "swaddling clothes." Glue "clothes" onto large heart.
7. Using fine-tip marker, draw lines on "robes."
8. Cut small hearts from foam sheets. Glue one on Mary, one on Joseph, and one on Jesus.
9. Cut star from foam sheet and glue onto gable of stable.
10. Glue pieces of straw onto stable.

11. After glue dries, use hole punch to make hole at the top. Thread ribbon through hole, then tie ends to form loop, or glue the keepsake onto a rock or film canister case for standing on desk or dresser.

Reflection

"Advent is concerned with that very connection between memory and hope, which is so necessary to the human person. Advent's intention is to awaken the most profound and basic emotional memory with us, namely, the memory of the God who became a child. This is a healing memory; it brings hope. The purpose of the Church's year is continually to rehearse her great history of memories, to awaken the heart's memory so that it can discern the star of hope....

Cardinal Joseph Ratzinger

Third Week of Advent

Popsicle Sticks Photo Frame

The gift of fond memories and loved ones, of times shared with others is a gift of love. Children can make this simple frame, and place one of their favorite photos in it and give it to a loved one. Instead of framing a photograph, children may choose to frame a picture they have drawn, which illustrates a Scripture verse about light.

Supplies needed:

8 popsicle or craft sticks

sturdy cardboard

craft glue

scissors

ruler

pencil

permanent markers (various colors)

beads, buttons, or other decorations

Directions:

1. Color Popsicle sticks with permanent markers. Let dry.

2. Measure a 6 by 6 inch square of cardboard and cut it out. Form outline of "frame" on the cardboard with 4 popsicle sticks.

3. Glue sticks into place, applying glue to entire length of sticks which will form the sides and bottom of frame. Because you will be sliding the photo under the stick at the top of the frame, apply glue only to the ends of that stick. Repeat process.

4. Glue beads, buttons, or other decorations to corners of frame.

5. Use fine-tip markers to write special message on the frame, such as "Friends Forever," "Best Mom," "I Love You," or the selected Scripture verse.

6. Cut a 3 inch triangle from another piece of cardboard. You'll use this for the "stand" in the back of your frame. Fold triangle in half lengthwise. Glue folded triangle to back of frame. Place weight on triangle until glue is dry.

7. Once glue dries, slide photo or drawing under popsicle sticks at the top of the frame and give as a gift.

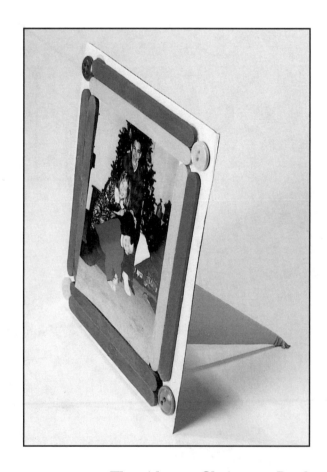

Potato-Stamp Note Cards

Easy

Make one-of-a-kind recipe cards for your favorite "baker" or "chef" using index cards, potatoes, and paints! Or make one-of-a-kind note cards for family and friends.

Supplies needed:

raw potatoes

paring knife

pencil

acrylic paints, available at craft stores

pie tins or paper plates

blank note cards with envelopes

index cards

paper towels

newspapers

red and green ribbon or yarn

Directions:

Note: Younger artists will need the help of an adult to carve the potato.

1. Spread newspapers over "work station" and "drying station."

2. Slice potato in half lengthwise.

3. Draw a simple design like a heart, star, or Christmas tree onto flat surface of potato with pencil.

4. Trim away potato from design, cutting to a depth of at least 3/8 inch deep around edges of design.

5. Pour paints into pie tins or paper plates, then line up several index cards or note cards on the newspaper in front of you, assembly line fashion.

6. Dip potato "stamp" into paint, gently press "stamp" onto paper towel to get rid of excess paint, then press "stamp" onto card(s).

7. Move wet cards from "work station" to "drying station." Repeat step 6. When cards are dry, bundle them together and tie with red and green ribbons or yarn.

Wreath Treats

The custom of decorating the home with wreaths at Christmas time originated in Northern Europe where there are many pine trees. The wreath, formed with evergreens such as pine, has long been a symbol of eternity.

These tasty mini-wreaths can serve as a symbol of life everlasting, the gift given us through the gift of Jesus, our Savior and Lord. The cinnamon candies symbolize the flames of burning candles. They remind us of Jesus, the Light of the World.

Ingredients:

1/3 cup margarine

1 10 oz. pkg. marshmallows

1 tsp. green food coloring

6 cups corn flakes

red cinnamon candies

prepared vanilla frosting (add green
    food coloring if desired)

non-stick cooking spray

wax paper

Directions:

1. Melt margarine in large saucepan over low heat. Once margarine is melted, add marshmallows. Stir until everything is completely melted. Remove pan from heat.

2. Stir in green food coloring. Make sure food coloring is mixed evenly so entire mixture is the same color.

3. Add corn flakes. Stir until corn flakes are coated with the margarine/marshmallow mixture.

4. Coat a 1/4 measuring cup with cooking spray. Scoop mixture into measuring cup and then onto wax paper. Coat your fingers with margarine and shape the 1/4 cup of mix into a wreath. Continue to measure out a 1/4 cup of mixture, re-coating measuring cup as needed, and making wreaths until there is no mixture left.

5. Place cinnamon candies on wreath for decoration, using a little of the prepared frosting to hold them in place.

Traditions create memories. Memories enrich our lives. Traditions help us pass on valuable lessons to our children and our children's children.

Candlelight

"God sent a man named John, who came to tell about the light and to lead all people to have faith. John wasn't that light...The true light that shines on everyone was coming into the world" (Jn 1:6–9).

For many families, the lighting of the Advent wreath candles is one of the most significant traditional customs practiced during Advent.

Most families find that the dinner hour is the perfect time to take part in this tradition. Some families emphasize the symbolism of this custom by dimming the lights in the room while the Advent wreath candles are lit. Following the Advent wreath ceremony, the overhead lights are turned back on. Night after night the darkened room is illuminated by candlelight. Week after week the candlelight continues to grow. This simple custom commemorates the many years the Israelites waited for Christ to come.

Some parishes begin their Sunday liturgies during Advent in much the same manner. During the four weeks of Advent parishioners enter the church on Sunday to find it darkened. The glimmer of Advent wreath candles welcomes the congregation. As verses of *O Come, O Come Emmanuel* are sung, the overhead lights gradually brighten. As the church is transformed from darkness to light, its members are reminded that Christ calls us to carry his light into the world.

Some families and parishes add a fifth white candle to their Advent wreath. This white candle, placed in the center of the wreath, is known as the Christmas candle. (Directions for making a Christmas candle are found in Week Four, page 84.) It is lit on Christmas Eve. It symbolizes that Christ, the Light of the World, is in our midst. And the celebration begins!

Stars

"Where is the child born to be king of the Jews? We saw his star in the east and have come to worship him" (Mt 2:2)

Some families hold the simple custom of hanging a single star in one of their front windows. It reminds young children that the wise men followed a special star in the sky to the place where Jesus was born. This single star in the window is a symbol that Jesus dwells within that home.

What makes the star more than a nice decoration for your home is its meaning. It is more than a decoration, it is a true symbol of Christ, our guiding star. It is important for children to be taught the meanings of our symbols. In addition to hanging the star in your window, make an event of it by coming together and reading a story or a piece of Scripture that will help children understand the symbol you are using in your window. And then, have a small discussion about the symbolism of the star. (You may also wish to watch *Little Drummer Boy* together.)

Luminaries

Many families enjoy the custom of placing luminaries along their sidewalks or driveways, or along the walk leading to their front door. The luminaries commemorate the plight of the Holy Family more than 2,000 years ago, when they searched in vain for a room at an inn in Bethlehem where they might rest for the night.

Today families use luminaries to signify that there is room for the Holy Family to dwell at their "inn."

Supplies needed:

wide-mouth, quart-size canning jars or
    gallon-size plastic milk jugs

sand

medium sized funnel

votive candles

fireplace matches or candle taper

utility knife

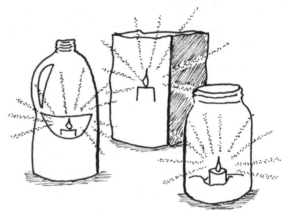

Directions:

For luminaries made from plastic milk jugs:

1. Wash and rinse milk jugs.

2. Slice a "smile" into each milk jug on the side opposite the handle. The slit should be made 3 inches from bottom of jug.

3. Pour sand through top of jug using funnel to fill the bottom with at least 1 inch of sand.

4. Lift "flap" of "smile" to place candle into sand.

5. Place luminaries along sidewalk and driveway, spacing every 3 feet or so, all the way up to your front door.

6. Light candles. Leave milk lids off so smoke and heat can escape.

For luminaries made from glass canning jars:

1. Pour enough sand into jars to fill bottoms of jars 1 inch deep with sand.

2. Place votive candles in center of sand. Shift sand around candle to hold candle in place.

Reflection

This Advent we look to the wise men to teach us where to focus our attention. We set our sights on things above, where God is. We draw closer to Jesus.... When our Advent journey ends, and we reach the place where Jesus resides in Bethlehem, may we, like the wise men, fall on our knees and adore him as our true and and only King.

Mark Zimmerman

Note: Start saving milk jugs at the beginning of the Advent season so you'll have enough to line your sidewalk, driveway and/or front walk to your door.

Third Week of Advent

Take-home pages offer some family activities that support what we are learning at school. We'd like you to consider choosing a few of these activities that you can share with your child and family at home.

Take one or two nights this week to share with your family the growing anticipation of this Advent season. Plan early in the week the evenings you will come together to participate in these activities. Also decide ahead of time which activity you will do on a night.

Some of the activities call for quiet reflection; some require an activity or project. Please read over the entire handout to see if advance planning is needed for any of the activities you choose to do.

During the first week of Advent we spent our time in hopeful waiting. During the second week of Advent we continued to prepare our hearts for the Lord. During this, the third week of Advent, we focus on rejoicing in Christ and carrying his light into the world.

The following activities are designed to help your family carry Christ's light into the world.

Warm-Up Exercises

1. Gather around the Advent wreath. Ask members of the family to light two purple candles plus the pink one. Read the following passage from Scripture:

You used to be like people living in the dark, but now you are people of the light because you belong to the Lord. So act like people of the light and make your light shine (Eph 5:8–9).

2. Tell your family to think of someone who lets his/her light shine.

Then ask them:

How does he/she let his/her light shine? Is it something he says/something she does?

Has that person helped you come to know Jesus a little bit better? Was it something he/she said or did?

Have you ever thanked that person for sharing the "light" with you? You should. We all need encouraging words.

3. As a family, take time to thank one another for sharing the "light." Brainstorm various ways to thank those who have shared the "light" with you. Here are a few "thank you" suggestions to get you started:

Call the person

Send a little note or card

Send a quick e-mail or e-card

Make a little magnet with your words of thanks (see page 62)

Getting Started...

1. You can let your light shine by the choices you make. So why not make a family commitment to support an issue, project, or service that carries Christ's light into the world? It could start at home with everyday choices regarding the magazines you read, the video games you play, the TV programs you watch.

2. Ask your family to name their favorite TV programs, movies, books, magazines, music, video games, and internet sites. Now, as a family, think about how much light these add to the world. Do some of the values espoused in these media bring more darkness than light? Make a family commitment to support only those media that make the world a brighter place!

3. Explore some of the following kid-friendly, family-friendly websites with your

children. If you don't have internet access at home, visit the local library. Here are a few sites you may want to explore:

My Friend Magazine (myfriendmagazine.com)

Guideposts for Kids (www.christianityinternational.com/guidepostsforkids.html)

Adventure Odyssey's website: Whit's End (www.whitsend.org)

The Kids Page (thekidzpage.com)

A Kids Heart (akidsheart.com)

Family Communications (Familycommunications.com)

God's World News (gwnews.com)

Bible Gateway (biblegateway.com)

Putting It into Practice...

1. Gather your family around the Advent wreath. Light two purple candles plus the pink one. Read the following from Scripture:

The Lord has chosen and sent me to tell the oppressed the good news, to heal the brokenhearted, and to announce freedom to prisoners and captives.... The LORD has sent me to comfort those who mourn.... He sent me to give them flowers in place of their sorrow, olive oil in place of their tears, and joyous praise in place of broken hearts (Is 61:1-3).

2. Discuss as a family how you can carry Christ's light into the world. You may want to consider....

Writing to your legislators in support of right-to-life issues, social justice issues, environmental issues, peaceful resolutions rather than war.

Donating Bibles or Christian reading materials to inmates at state prisons.

Sponsoring a child in a Third World country, so he or she can have at least his or her most basic needs met.

Helping a family-in-need anonymously through "The Giving Tree" program at church. On each of the presents attach a card that says something such as "From Someone Who Cares" or "From a Friend in Christ" or "Jesus Cares and So Do We."

3. Decide on something your family can do this Advent (or better still, an on-going commitment) to bring Christ's light into the world, and then do it with joyful hearts!

Reflection

As Advent draws closer to Christmas, the advertisements remind us daily how many shopping days there are till Christmas. Now would be a good time to find out the scheduled times of the Christmas liturgies in your parish. Perhaps as a family you can choose the Christmas Mass you wish to attend and schedule breakfast and opening presents around that time. If presents are going to be opened after Mass, have a small religious gift ready that you can give each child on the way to Mass. This is a tradition that kids catch on to with enthusiasm, and each year they will wait for that "special gift" they get on the way to Christmas Mass.

Sr. Kathryn James Hermes, FSP

Fourth Week of Advent

The theme for the fourth week of Advent is love—God's love for us and our love for God and others.

Week Four holds ideas for last-minute preparations for the coming Christmas celebrations. Simple kitchen activities and gift wrapping ideas are included here. Because the final week of Advent can be hectic, the Take-Home page does not contain activities for the family to do. Rather, it suggests simple prayers that can be incorporated into your Christmas celebrations.

As with all weeks of Advent, please glance through this section so you are familiar with the week's activities. Some will require advance planning to give you time to round up needed supplies. If you're planning to use luminaries on Christmas Eve, you may want to assemble them at the beginning of the week. If you're holding a "Birthday Party for Jesus" you'll need to take care of last-minute details now. See the "Birthday Party" section beginning on page 93. Also, flip to the back of the book to find reproducible puzzles and games that will come in handy for "quiet-time" activities in an otherwise hectic week.

The fourth week of Advent ends on Christmas day.

Week-at-a-Glance

Where Are All

By Niki Schoenfeldt
Illustrated by Chuck Galey

As I stood beside the Christmas tree staring out the window at the cold snowless night, I noticed the nice round shrubs huddled against the house. Mom had planted them when we moved in a few years ago. Because the cold of winter had turned everything else in the yard brown, the evergreeens really stood out in the moonlight. The weather wasn't the only thing cold this Christmas Eve. There was an icy coldness in my heart, too. This would be our first Christmas without Mom. Daddy, my brother James and I were finishing up the decorating, but since Mom died, all the decorating in the world couldn't make me smile.

"Come help me hang the stockings, Beth," I heard James say to me, as he surveyed the hooks that he had hung on the mantle.

I turned away from the window and dug through one of the boxes scattered about our living room floor. In it I found our stockings. Mom had written our names on each one of them with glitter. Beside each name was her trademark smiley face. Mom couldn't write anything without putting a smiley face next to it! Even the sandwiches she put in my lunchbox had smiley faces etched onto the bread! She would always say, "A smile is a gift from God."

Dad came in with another box of decorations. "I think the star is in this one, Beth. Want to put it on the tree?"

"No thanks," I said as I dropped my stocking back into the box and headed for my room. I didn't feel like decorating any more.

A few minutes later, as I crawled into bed, there was a knock at my door. It was James.

"What's wrong, Beth?" he asked, as he sat down beside me. "Don't you want to get ready for Christmas?"

"I don't want Christmas," I said. "I want MOM! I miss her so much. I miss her smiley faces. Where are all the smiles now?"

he Smiles Now?

"They're right here," he said, giving me his silliest grin and pointing to himself. "Mom is still with us, Beth. She's in me and she's in you. She is part of us. We are the best smiley faces that she ever made!"

I smiled at him. He was right. She had taught us all to smile, and she did enjoy our smiling faces. "I just want to sleep now, James. Maybe I can spend Christmas with Mom in my dreams."

"I'm sure you will, Sis," he said, as he hugged me goodnight. "Special things tend to happen on Christmas Eve. It's the night of miracles!" He turned off the light and shut the door as he left.

I pulled the covers up around me to ward off the chill. Would a miracle happen tonight? If only... I thought, and a tear slipped down my cheek and onto my pillow.

That night I had the most wonderful dreams. I dreamt that Mom was helping us trim the tree and that she clapped and cheered when Daddy lifted me to put the star on top. It was snowing outside and we were all snuggled by the fire listening to Christmas carols on the stereo. I sat next to Mom and we swayed to the music...

That morning when I woke up, I could see tiny flakes of snow falling lazily past my bedroom window. I could hear the faint sound of Christmas carols playing from the living room. It reminded me of my dream. Wistfully, I thought that maybe it wasn't a dream after all! I jumped out of bed and ran down the hall toward the music. There, looking out the window beside the Christmas tree, were Daddy and James.

"Oh," I said, stopping short when I saw them. "I thought Mom was here. I guess it was just a dream."

"Maybe she was here," said Dad, motioning me toward the window. "Come see." I slowly padded my way toward the window in my bare feet and when I looked outside, I could hardly believe my eyes! The snow on top of the hedges had formed little white circles, and on top of each one, a smiley face had been painted in the snow! A dozen little gifts from God!

"Oh, my," I whispered, "she really was here."

"She's still with us; I told you that," said James, as he gave Daddy a wink.

That little wink had given him away. At that moment I knew that James had painted those smiley faces in the snow for me.

"You're right, James," I laughed. "She's in me and she's in YOU!" I reached over to wrap him in a big bear hug. James had made my Christmas miracle that morning but I knew that somehow, with the help of Jesus, Mom had told him what to do.

Though Christmas is a joyful time for many people, it can be difficult for those who have lost loved ones. Think of something you can do for a family who is spending their first Christmas without one of their loved ones. Let them know you care. Brighten their day with a thoughtful gesture or a simple gift of love.

Snow paint a special Christmas gift for someone you love! Fill empty spray bottles with water and put a few drops of food coloring in each. (You'll need as many bottles as colors you want to paint.) Then paint pictures in the snow. Make snow sculptures and paint them, too!

Reprinted from *My Friend—A Catholic Magazine for Kids*, Pauline Books & Media, 50 Saint Pauls Avenue, Boston, MA 02130. www.myfriendmagazine.com

Advent Wreath Ceremony

The Advent wreath symbolizes our time of waiting, our time of hoping. It helps us mark our days until Christmas.

This Advent wreath ceremony provides you with an opportunity to pass on tradition, to share Scripture and prayer, and to help children understand that Christ is at the center of our days of waiting.

The ceremony takes only minutes, making it easy to incorporate into busy days. One person reads the Scripture passage, another reads the prayer, another lights the candle, then everyone joins in with the response.

Remember that the fourth week of Advent may not last seven days. Use this handout for the remaining days of Advent. On Christmas Eve you can light a center white candle, a Christmas candle (page 84) and read a selection from the Christmas Gospel. (Do not leave burning candles unattended.)

Micah 5:2

Bethlehem Ephrathah,
you are one of the smallest towns
in the nation of Judah.
But the LORD will choose
one of your people
to rule the nation—
someone whose family
goes back to ancient times.

Reader:

As we light our final candle,
we know that Advent
is coming to an end.

Soon we will celebrate the birth of Jesus, our Savior and our friend!

Light all four candles.

All:

Come, Jesus, Savior of the world.
Come, Lord Jesus, come.

Isaiah 7:10; 13; 14

Once again the LORD God spoke to king Ahaz....
Listen, every one of you, in the royal family of
David. The LORD will still give you proof. A vir-
gin is pregnant; she will have a son and will
name him Immanuel.

Reader:

> Lord God,
> thank you for sending us your prophets.
> Thank you for Mary,
> the mother of your Son.
> Thank you for Jesus,
> our Lord and our Savior.
> Thank you, Lord God, Emmanuel!
> Amen.

> *Light all four candles.*

All:

> Come, Jesus, Savior of the world.
> Come, Lord Jesus, come.

Luke 1:26, 27, 30–33

God sent the angel Gabriel to the town of Nazareth in Galilee with a message for a virgin named Mary.... Then the angel told Mary, "Don't be afraid! God is pleased with you, and you will have a son. His name will be Jesus. He will be great and will be called the Son of God Most High. The Lord God will make him king, as his ancestor David was. He will rule the people of Israel forever and his kingdom will never end."

Leader:

> Lord God,
> may we, like Mary,
> welcome your Word
> into our hearts
> and carry your love
> into the world.
> Amen.

Light all four candles.

All:

> Come, Jesus, Savior of the world.
> Come, Lord Jesus, come.

Luke 1:38

Mary said, "I am the Lord's servant! Let it happen as you have said."

Leader:

> Dear God,
> you sent your special messenger to Mary
> to deliver the good news.
> She trusted in you with all her heart.
> Help us to learn to trust like Mary.
> Help us learn to listen
> and follow your Word.
> Amen.

> *Light all four candles.*

All:

> Come, Jesus, Savior of the World.
> Come, Lord Jesus, come.

Matthew 1:20–21

The angel said, "Joseph, the baby that Mary will have is from the Holy Spirit. Go ahead and marry her. Then after the baby is born, name him Jesus, because he will save his people from their sins."

Reader:

Dear God,
sometimes it's hard for me
to do what you want me to do.
Help me to be like
Jesus, Mary, and Joseph
and follow your heavenly will.
Amen.

Light all four candles.

All:

Come, Jesus, Savior of the world.
Come, Lord Jesus, come.

Psalm 89:1–2

Our Lord, I will sing of your love forever. Everyone yet to be born will hear me praise your faithfulness. I will tell them, "God's love can always be trusted, and his faithfulness lasts as long as the heavens."

Reader:

Dear Lord, we know
that you truly love us.
You sent us your only Son.
Today and every day
of our lives
we will celebrate the gift
of your love
as we celebrate
the gift of your Son!
Amen.

Light all four candles.

All:

Come, Jesus, Savior of the world.
Come, Lord Jesus, come.

Matthew 1:22–23

So the Lord's promise came true, just as the prophet had said, "A virgin will have a baby boy and he will be called Immanuel," which means "God is with us."

Reader:

Lord God,
thank you for keeping
your promise.
Thank you
for sending your Son
into the world.
We know that you
are with us always,
Lord God Emmanuel!
Amen.

Light all four candles.

All:

Come, Jesus, Savior of the world.
Come, Lord Jesus, come.

Bird Feeders

As St. Francis of Assisi incorporated nature into the first live nativity scene, we, too, can include nature in our Advent activities.

This craft will help children remember that as stewards of the earth we are called to lovingly care for our environment and animals. The added gift of the kindness done to these little animals by making these easy bird feeders is to see them flock to your yard!

Pinecone Bird Feeder

Easy

Supplies needed:

pine cones   ribbon
bird seed   wax paper
peanut butter

Directions:

1. Cover the work surface with the wax paper.
2. Spread peanut butter all over a pine cone then roll it in birdseed until covered with seeds.
3. Tie a ribbon around the top of the pinecone and tie end to form a loop. Tie the pinecone "bird feeder" to the branch of a tree.

Mesh Bag Bird Feeder

Easy

Supplies needed:

small, plastic mesh bag (the type that holds onions or garlic)
variety of unshelled, unsalted nuts. (For an extra special treat, fill the mesh bag with a variety of fresh nuts: walnuts, hazelnuts, pecans, unsalted peanuts and almonds.)
large bowl   cord

Directions:

1. Place nuts in bowl and mix.
2. Fill mesh bag with mixed nuts.
3. Tie bag closed with cord. Hang your bird feeder on a tree and watch the birds arrive! Nuts also attract squirrels so keep a stash of acorns, chestnuts, hickory nuts, and beechnuts handy for feeding your furry friends.

Apple Bird Feeder

Supplies needed:

apples   ribbon
unsalted sunflower
seeds

Directions:

1. Core an apple (remove the center of the apple).
2. Poke sunflower seeds into apple, placing them close together.
3. Thread ribbon through core hole in apple and tie to a tree branch. Sunflower seeds will attract chickadees, cardinals, titmice, nuthatches, juncos, mourning doves, and jays. Happy bird watching!

Note: Some bird feeding tips can be found on page 83.

Garland for Critters and Birds

Another way for children to acquire an appreciation for animals is to decorate an outdoor tree with tasty treats for both furry and feathered friends.

Supplies needed:

sewing needle

buttonhole thread (a strong thread that can be found at most stores where fabrics are sold)

brightly colored ribbons or yarns

Plus a combination of the following:

plain, unsalted popcorn

cranberries

rosehips

dried fruits

mini marshmallows

stale bread

stale bagels

carrots

apples (yellow, green and red)

peanuts, in shell, no salt

unbaked pastry dough

Directions:

1. Gather supplies.
2. Cut:
   apples into chunks (leave skins on. Use yellow, red, and green apples for greater color)
   carrots into 1/4 inch thick slices
   stale bread into 1/2 inch cubes
   stale bagels into 1/2 inch slices.
3. Roll left-over pastry dough into marble-sized balls.
4. Thread needle with buttonhole thread that is at least 3 feet long.
5. Poke needle through first ingredient. Gently slide ingredient to within 1 1/2 inches from end of thread. Tie a knot around first ingredient to keep ingredients from falling off.
6. Continue adding a variety of ingredients until thread is nearly full. Set this section aside. Repeat steps 4–6 until you have enough strands to decorate your tree. Tie 3 foot sections together, forming one continuous strand.
7. Tie red, yellow, and orange ribbon or yarn here and there to garland. These colorful additions will attract birds and supply building materials for spring nests!
8. Drape garland on a tree.

A Few Bird Feeding Tips

Place bird feeders and garlands in trees found on the south side of your house where they will be more protected from cold, northern winds.

Choose a tree near a window so you can enjoy watching the birds feed.

Once you start feeding birds, continue to replenish your bird feeders and/or garland throughout the cold, winter months. The birds will keep coming back for more!

Christmas Candle

Once Christmas Eve arrives Advent is over and the Christmas season has begun. To mark the change of seasons, make this Christmas candle that can be lit on Christmas Eve and throughout the Christmas season. Transform your Advent wreath into a Christmas wreath by replacing the purple and pink candles with white tapers and place this Christmas candle in the center. Your Advent wreath becomes a Christmas wreath. When all the candles are lit they will remind children that Jesus loves us so much that he came to us to light the way to heaven. This Christmas candle is so-o-o easy to make and filled with symbolism to share with children. (Adult supervision will be needed to melt parafin.)

Supplies needed:

quart-sized cardboard milk carton
10" wick (can be purchased at most
   craft stores)
pencil
ruler
2 lb. box of paraffin (can be purchased
   at most craft stores)
double boiler
scissors
permanent marker

Directions:

1. Using permanent marker measure 7 inches from the bottom of the milk carton. Trim your milk carton to measure 7 inches tall.

2. Tie wick to center of pencil. Place pencil on top of opened carton with wick dangling inside.

3. Melt paraffin in double boiler. Do not overheat the wax. When the wax has completely melted, remove top part of the double boiler.

4. Pour the melted wax into mold. As soon as the wax sets completely, tear carton from candle.

5. Place candle in center of Advent wreath, or place candle on saucer surrounded by evergreens and use as a centerpiece on your table for Christmas day. (Never leave a lit candle unattended or in a room where children are unattended. Be sure that the evergreens are not near the candle flame.)

Gift Wrap

Every act of kindness is a gift of love. After the children have made (or bought) gifts to be given to family and/or donated to others in need, they can present their gifts in handmade gift wrapping. See simple packaging ideas below and on page 86. Making your own gift wrap is as easy as 1-2-3!

Finger Painted Gift Wrap

Easy

Supplies needed:

finger paints (various colors)
sturdy plastic plates or Styrofoam™ trays
finger paint paper   newspaper

Directions:

1. Cover "work station" and "drying station" with plenty of newspaper.

2. Pour finger paints onto plates or Styrofoam™ trays. Use one color per plate/tray.

3. Children dip their fingers into the paint and create their own masterpiece! Children can "paint" wiggly-squiggly lines, "write" their own Christmas greetings with their fingers, or draw symbols of the season all over the paper.

4. Place finished gift wrap on newspapers at the drying station until they are completely dry.

Blow-Your-Own Gift Wrap

Supplies needed:

tissue paper (white)
food coloring (various colors)
drinking straws   newspapers

Directions:

1. Cover "work station" and "drying station" with newspaper.

2. Each child receives his/her own drinking straw. There should be no sharing of straws.

3. Squeeze a few drops of desired liquid food coloring onto tissue paper and begin to blow on it through the straw. By blowing hard and fast through the straw starburst patterns will form. By blowing slowly and softly through the straw, thick, squiggly lines will form.

4. Children continue to add drops of food coloring until they are satisfied with their designs. Caution children if they try to add color upon color the tissue paper will begin to come apart.

5. Place the one-of-a-kind wrapping paper to dry on the newspaper at the drying station.

6. If wrinkles form, press tissue paper with dry iron (set on lowest setting). Children will need adult supervision or have an adult do the ironing.

Tip: Make sure you spread lots of newspaper over your "work station" and your "drying station." Wear an apron or a "paint" shirt while you and the children create the gift wrap.

Gift Bags

For those hard-to-wrap gifts, make your own special bags from lunch bags or other plain paper bags.

For older artists

Supplies needed:

paper lunch bags (or other plain paper bags, any size, any color)

acrylic or poster paints (various colors, not the same color as the bags)

pie tins or paper plates

sponges

scissors

construction paper

permanent markers

newspaper

Directions:

1. Spread newspaper over work station. Pour paints into pie tins or paper plates.

2. Cut sponge to form a holly leaf (or any other seasonal design desired).

3. Wet sponge to soften it, then squeeze excess water from sponge.

4. Dip dampened sponge into paint then "stamp" bag with sponge. To form small details, such as berries, dip fingertips into paint and dab paint onto bags. Let dry.

5. When dry, fold top of bag down toward stamped design.

6. Cut strip of construction paper and glue to open edge of bag.

7. With permanent marker write "To:" and "From:" on strip of construction paper.

For younger artists

Supplies needed:

paper lunch bags (or other plain paper bags any size, any color)

finger paints (various colors, not the same color as the bags)

pie tins or paper plates

markers   newspaper

Directions:

1. Spread newspaper on work station.

2. Pour paints into pie tins or paper plates.

3. Lay several bags side by side on newspaper.

4. Dip hands into paints, then press handprints onto bags.

5. To form hearts, dip thumbs into paint, then overlap thumb prints on bag. Let paints dry.

6. Fold top of bag down toward handprint.

7. Write "To:" and "From:" on bag with marker.

Sugar Cookies

The process of baking cookies provides the perfect opportunity for teaching a lesson about the Body of Christ. Explain to your children or students that the taste of flour by itself isn't very nice, nor is the idea of eating a raw egg very appealing. But by coming together all the ingredients, with their own individuality, become a part of something truly delicious. That's the way it is with being members of the loving Body of Christ. We come together and project together the love of God in the world.

Baking cookies is also a great activity because it can involve people of all ages. Younger children can mix, stir, roll, and cut, while older ones help "supervise" the younger ones plus help with the baking. Everyone can help with frosting the cookies!

Supplies needed:

large mixing bowl
cookie cutters (seasonal shapes)
rolling pin   mixer
cookie sheets   wire cookie racks

Ingredients:

1 cup (2 sticks) margarine (at room temperature)
1 cup granulated sugar
1 egg
2 tsp. baking powder
1 tsp. vanilla
1/2 tsp. almond extract
3 cups flour

Directions:

1. Preheat oven to 400°. Put margarine and sugar in a large mixing bowl. With a mixer combine margarine and sugar until they are creamy.

You may need to stop the mixer a few times to scrape the sides of the bowl until all the margarine and sugar are blended together.

2. Add egg, vanilla, and almond extract and mix until well blended.

3. Sprinkle baking powder over mixture, then add flour one cup at a time until all flour is added. The dough will be stiff.

4. Sprinkle flour on counter to keep dough from sticking, then roll dough to 1/4 inch thickness. Use cookie cutters to cut dough and place on cookie sheet about 1 inch apart.

5. Bake for 6 to 7 minutes at 400° or until golden in color. Remove cookies from cookie sheets and cool on wire cookie racks.

Frosting for cookies

Ingredients:

2 cups powdered sugar
1 tbsp. butter
1/2 tsp. almond extract
dash of salt
enough milk to make frosting creamy
food coloring
colored sugar

Directions:

1. Combine all the ingredients except the colored sugar into medium size bowl. Mix until well blended.

2. Divide frosting into small bowls, add desired food coloring and stir until color is even.

3. Spread frosting onto cooled cookies then sprinkle with colored sugar.

Fourth Week of Advent

Trail Mix

Easy

These tasty treats (pages 88–89) make great gifts or they can be made ahead of time to welcome family and friends who will visit during the Christmas season. This trail mix has a bit of everything in it. Fruit, cereal, nuts, crackers, pretzels, and chocolates! Mmmm, Mmmm, good!

Supplies needed:

1/2 cup mini pretzels
3/4 cup red and green candy coated
    chocolate pieces
1/2 cup salted peanuts
1/2 cup mini cheese crackers
1/2 cup raisins
1 cup rice cereal squares
any other similar snack items you have at
    home
small plastic bags
red and green ribbon or yarn

Directions:

1. Measure and pour all ingredients into a medium size plastic bowl that has a matching lid.
2. Seal with lid.
3. Shake well to mix ingredients.
4. Pour mix into small plastic bags and tie with red and green ribbon or yarn.
5. Give as gifts to friends who come to visit.

Candy Tree

Easy

Make a centerpiece that's sweet to eat!

Supplies needed:

1 Styrofoam™ cone, 10"–12" tall
straight pins
individually wrapped hard candies,
    in assorted colors and/or wrappers
Optional: mini bow

Directions:

1. On the top of the Stryofoam™ cone pin one piece of hard candy. Make sure to pin both ends of the wrapper to the Styrofoam™.
2. Work your way down the cone, pinning rows of candy. Use a variety of colors to give the tree a colorful look.
3. The "twisty" ends of the candies should run vertically on the tree in all rows except the bottom row which runs horizontally. (The candies hang better that way.)
4. Optional: Attach a mini bow to the top of the tree.

Reflection

This is Christmas: not the tinsel, not the giving and receiving, not even the carols, but the humble heart that receives anew the wondrous gift, the Christ.

Frank McKibben

Peppermint Bark

Three ingredients equal a delicious gift!

Supplies needed:

9" x 9" baking pan   meat mallet
wax paper   double boiler
plastic cling wrap

Ingredients:

1 lb. white chocolate, available in slab or miniature discs (can be found in finer grocery stores and in craft stores that sell candy making supplies)

1/4 tsp. peppermint oil (can be found in finer grocery stores and in craft stores that sell candy making supplies)

6 large candy canes

Directions:

1. Line 9 by 9 inch baking pan with wax paper. This will prevent bark from sticking to the pan. Set aside till later.

2. If you have the chocolate in disc form, place these into the top of the double boiler. If you have a slab of chocolate, break chocolate into pieces first and then place into double boiler.

3. In top of double boiler, melt white chocolate. If you don't have a double boiler, place a metal bowl on top of a pot of simmering, NOT boiling, water. (Chocolate scorches easily.) AS SOON AS the chocolate is melted, remove pan from heat.

4. Wrap meat mallet with plastic cling wrap. This prevents any bacteria from the meat mallet from contaminating candy. Break candy canes into tiny pieces with covered meat mallet.

4. Stir peppermint pieces plus peppermint oil into melted chocolate.

5. Pour mixture into baking pan lined with wax paper. Chill in refrigerator for 30 minutes until "bark" is set.

6. Remove from refrigerator and break "bark" into pieces by hand. Package peppermint "bark" into jars or baggies, attach a ribbon and the recipe, and give as a gift!

Chocolate Dips

Easy to make! Yummy to eat! Great for gifts!

Supplies needed:

11" x 17" baking sheet   fork
wax paper   double boiler

Ingredients:

2 lbs. coating chocolate, available in slab or miniature discs (can be found in finer grocery stores and in craft stores that sell candy making supplies)

Any of the following foods to dip: pretzels, potato chips, dried apricots, fresh strawberries, marshmallows, graham crackers, peanut butter crackers, caramels

Directions:

1. Line 11 by 17 inch baking sheet with waxed paper. This is where you will place your "dipped" treats until chocolate sets.

2. In top of double boiler, melt chocolate. AS SOON AS chocolate is melted, remove from heat.

3. Partially dip pretzels, potato chips, dried apricots, or fresh strawberries (washed and dried with caps still on) into chocolate, then place on waxed paper to set.

4. Drop a few marshmallows, graham crackers, peanut butter crackers, pretzels, or caramels at a time into the chocolate. Use fork to dunk them until completely covered with chocolate, then scoop them out of the chocolate. Tap fork against side of pan or bowl to drain excess chocolate, then place on waxed paper to set.

5. Once completely set, place into sandwich bags, attach ribbon, and give as a gift!

Traditions create memories. Memories enrich our lives. Traditions also help us pass on valuable lessons to our children and our children's children.

Serving Others, Serving Christ

As the days of Advent wind to a close, we prepare for the coming celebrations. Some families begin their Christmas celebrations by serving breakfast or brunch to the poor and homeless on Christmas Eve or Christmas morning. This tradition of serving others before participating in any festivities is as much a part of their Christmas celebration as giving gifts to those they love.

The list of agencies and services that welcome family volunteers is endless—homeless shelters, soup kitchens, pregnancy care centers, nursing homes, family and children's services, the Salvation Army, Good Neighbors, Catholic Charities, the Christ Child Society, St. Vincent de Paul Society, among others, which are too many to list.

These agencies and shelters rely on volunteers year-round to help them provide basic necessities to those who walk through their doors. During the holiday season shelters, agencies, and services provide more than the basics to those who walk through their doors. They supply gifts for individuals and for their families—gifts that otherwise could not be given. Gloves and mittens, hats and scarves, socks and underwear, sweaters and flannel shirts are among the most common, yet needed gifts.

Each center, agency, or service has its own list of rules and requirements for volunteers, so check first to see if young children are welcome to volunteer.

Many soup kitchens and shelters allow youngsters to help set tables or fill "goodie bags" and "care packages" under the supervision of a parent. Others allow younger children to help distribute gifts to their guests. Some allow older children to carry food trays to tables, pour drinks for their guests, and clear tables after meals. So check first to see if your entire family can participate together.

If your children are too young to help out at a center, they can help you make some baked goods at home for the center. They can also help wrap the goodies and write special messages like "From someone who cares" or "Jesus loves you" or "God bless you" on gift tags. They can attach the tags to the packages of goodies. Then they can help to deliver them to a center or soup kitchen nearby.

When adults take the time to teach young children that reaching out to others in need is what we are all called to do, then children learn that faith involves action.

Reflection

"Luke's Gospel account of the Christmas event is full of activity...And yet, in the middle of the frenetic action, here is this woman wrapped in mystical silence...She demonstrates the necessity of a quiet place within ourselves at Christmastime—that place where we are most ourselves in relation to God. It is a place of silence, not because it is untouched by all the activity of our lives, but because it is capable of wonder. Every prayer begins with silent wonder before it turns to words. Our first response to God is dumbstruck awe at who he is and what he has done for us."

William Frebuger

Fourth Week of Advent

During the first week of Advent, we spent our time in watchful waiting. During the second week of Advent, we prepared our hearts for the coming of the Lord. During the third week of Advent, we rejoiced in Christ, the Light of the World. During this fourth week of Advent, we will focus on God's gift of love for us and our gift of love to him and others.

Because the last week of Advent can be a hectic one filled with Christmas parties, pageants, and programs, you may find it challenging to add more activities to your already long list of "Things to Do." For this reason, this week's activities include two simple prayers plus a page of coloring fun.

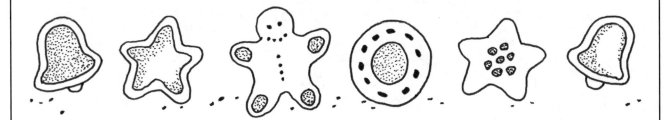

A Christmas Tree Blessing

As you gather to decorate your Christmas tree, take a moment to pray this simple blessing.

Dear Heavenly Father,
we ask you to bless our Christmas tree.
May it serve as a symbol of this special time of year.
May its evergreen branches remind us of the gift Jesus came to give: the gift of everlasting life.
May its ornaments remind us of the many blessings you grant us day after day, year after year.
And may its tree top star remind us that Jesus is the Light of the World.
This we pray in Jesus' name.
Amen.

A Christmas Meal Prayer

Heavenly Father, on this, your Son's birthday, we thank you for our many blessings, especially for the gift of your Son, Jesus, the Prince of Peace.

We ask you to bless this food that we are about to eat; and bless our loved ones, too, plus all of those who have gone before us in faith and all people everywhere.

May we, as followers of Jesus, carry your peace, love, and light into the world this Christmas and always.
Amen.

Advent Color-and-Search Challenge:
How many things can you find hidden in this picture?

Birthday Party for Jesus

The purpose for a "Birthday Party for Jesus" is twofold. It offers children a special way to celebrate the birth of Jesus, plus it helps children learn to reach out to others in need. In so doing, we are helping our children learn to live their faith through actions. Unlike other birthday parties, gifts brought to this party are donated to a charity of choice.

Because this time of year tends to hold a calendar full of activities, it's best to plan for this party well in advance. You may want to hold a "Birthday Party for Jesus" during the third week of Advent so that the gifts collected can be distributed to local agencies and charities in plenty of time for them to deliver the gifts to those in need.

Epiphany is another opportune day for holding a "Birthday Party for Jesus." Epiphany is the day we commemorate the Magi visiting the infant Jesus. A party on this day helps children realize that the season of Christmas doesn't end with opening gifts on Christmas morning.

Baby Jesus Birthday Party

Invitation to Jesus' Birthday Party

Please

come

to a

Birthday

Party!

For: **Jesus**

When: Epiphany Sunday, January 6

Where: My house
45 Heaven's Gate Road
Yondervalle, AR

Time: 2:00 P.M.—4:30 P.M.

Gifts will be donated in Jesus'
name to _Pro-Life Ministries_
after the party. Please check the
list of suggested items.

Suggested words to use for the inside of the invitation:

Please come to a Birthday Party!

For: Jesus

When: Epiphany Sunday (Include date.)

Where: My house. (Include your address.)

Time: From... To... (Plan on a few hours.)

Gifts will be donated in Jesus' name to (name of charity) after the party.

Please check the list of suggested items. (Make sure to include list.)

For Pregnancy Care Centers or Pro-Life Ministries

Suggested items include: Bibs, feeding bottles, teething rings, diapers, baby clothes, rattles, crib sheets, receiving blankets, afghans, socks, booties, baby lotion, and shampoo.

For Local Food Banks

Suggested items include: Peanut butter, jelly, spaghetti, noodles, pastas, rice, instant potato flakes, cans or jars of tomato sauces, canned soups, canned vegetables and fruits, canned tuna and meats, pudding, Jell-O™, flour, sugar, dessert mixes, toilet paper, paper towels, laundry detergent, dish detergent, and bars of soap.

For Soup Kitchens

Ask your guests to bring a tub of frosting and a jar of sprinkles so you can decorate cookies to donate to a soup kitchen. (You will supply the cookies. Sugar cookie recipe is found on page 87.)

For Shelters

Suggested items include: Hats, gloves, or mittens. Also ask your guests to bring a pair of sewing shears because you will be making fleece neck scarves to donate along with the hats, gloves, and mittens. (You will need to go to a fabric store and purchase the fleece, or ask someone to bring fleece with them to the party.)

Birthday Cake

This extra-special cake is not only tasty, but full of symbolism, too! Make sure you discuss with the children the meaning of the symbols used for this birthday cake. When you are ready to cut the cake use the Birthday Prayer to Jesus found on page 101.

- White, a symbol for purity, is the color of the topping and the cake.
- The single, white candle is a symbol for Jesus, the Light of the World.
- The evergreens arranged around the cake plate are a symbol for eternal life, our gift from Christ, our Savior and Lord.

Directions:

1. Thaw non-dairy whipped topping.
2. Place angel food cake onto cake plate.
3. Place candle holder in center of cake. Place candle into holder.
4. Spread thawed whipped topping over cake. If you are icing the cake ahead of time, store it in the refrigerator until you are ready to serve.
5. When ready to serve, arrange evergreens around the base of the plate.

Supplies needed:

1 store-bought angel food cake (or you can make one from scratch)

1 tub of non-dairy whipped topping (if your cake is very big, you may need a few tubs of topping)

cake plate

12" white taper candle or birthday candles and other decorations

candle holder

evergreen branches

Reflection

This Advent we look to the wise men to teach us where to focus our attention. We set our sights on things above, where God is. We draw closer to Jesus.... When our Advent journey ends, and we reach the place where Jesus resides in Bethlehem, may we, like the wise men, fall on our knees and adore him as our true and and only King.

Mark Zimmerman

Stick-the-Star-over-the-Stable

This game is played like "Pin-the-Tail-on-the-Donkey." If you would like the game to last from year to year, consider laminating the stable scene.

Supplies needed for stable scene:

1 piece of standard size blue poster board (22" x 28")

brown, yellow, and white construction paper

scissors   craft glue

Directions for making the stable scene:

1. On brown construction paper draw a stable. (See diagram for guide.) Cut out stable, then glue to blue poster board.

2. On yellow construction paper draw and then cut out the stable. Glue to stable.

3. On white construction paper draw and then cut out several stars, enough for each of your guests. Do not glue these on.

4. Take one star and trace it with a marker over the stable. This will be your "designated spot" where the children will try to place their star.

Supplies needed for playing the game:

stable scene   markers

blindfold   star for every child

sticky-tack or masking tape for each star

Directions for playing the game:

1. Each child picks a star and writes his/her name on it.

2. One child at a time is blindfolded, spun around a few times, then turned to face the "stable."

3. The child approaches the "stable" with one hand behind his/her back. Holding his/her star in the other hand, the child places it in the sky above the "stable" wherever initial contact is made.

4. The blindfold is then removed so the child can see how close he/she came to the "right" spot. Once everyone has had a turn, the child who placed the star closest to the designated spot wins.

No Room at the Inn

This game is played like "Musical Chairs."

Before the party:

Using markers, write "NO ROOM" on several sheets of construction paper. You will be attaching these "signs" to the chairs you'll be using during the "No Room at the Inn" game.

During the party:

Supplies needed:

chairs   CD/cassette player

Christmas music

"NO ROOM" signs for chairs

sticky tack or masking tape

Directions for playing the game:

1. To determine the number of chairs you will need, count the number of participants in the game minus one.

2. Gather the chairs you will need. Place them back-to-back, forming two rows. Attach the "NO ROOM" signs to the backs of the chairs with masking tape or sticky tack.

3. Have guests stand around the chairs.

4. Start Christmas music. As music plays, guests walk along "their journey to Bethlehem." When you stop the music, everyone scrambles to find "a room at the inn." The one that did not find "a room at the inn" is out of the game.

5. Remove one chair from the rows of chairs and repeat the process. Continue until one person is sitting on the final chair. This person wins the game.

Reflection

"Take time to be aware that in the very midst of our busy preparations for the celebration of Christ's birth in ancient Bethlehem, Christ is reborn in the Bethlehems of our homes and daily lives. Take time, slow down, be still, be awake to the Divine Mystery that looks so common and so ordinary yet is wonderously present.... The supreme trick of Old Scratch is to have us so busy decorating, preparing food, practicing music, and cleaning in preparation for the feast of Christmas that we actually miss the coming of Christ. Hurt feelings, anger, impatience, injured egos— the list of clouds that busyness creates to blind us to the birth can be long, but it is familiar to us all."

Edward Hays

Guess the Number

This is a simple guessing game where guests try to estimate the number of pieces of straw in the manger.

Supplies needed:

small box

brown and yellow construction paper

scissors

pencil or marker

ruler

glue or stapler

Directions:

Before the party:

1. Make a mini-manger out of a small box. (A baby shoebox is perfect!) To do this, cover box with brown construction paper.

2. Make "straw" for the manger from yellow construction paper. Cut strips 1/2 inch wide by 6 inches long. Crumple paper "straw."

3. Fill manger with crumpled "straw."

4. Now remove "straw" from manger and count the "straw."

5. Write that number on a small piece of paper and tape to the bottom of the manger, with number face down so it can't be seen. Return "straw" to manger.

During the party:

1. Gather guests around "manger." Pass out paper and pens to guests. Ask guests to estimate the number of "straw" in the manger and write that number on his/her sheet of paper.

2. Next, have guests show their numbers to you.

3. Then remove "straw" from manger and take the number from the bottom of the manger and show it to your guests.

4. Whoever guesses the right number — or comes closest to the number without exceeding it — wins the game.

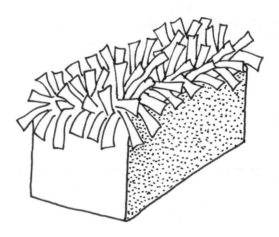

Reflection

Christmas is about children. Certainly Mary must have known that in a particular way that first Christmas morn. But we too, when we have time to touch the deepest chords of Christmas in our hearts, know that this season is known most truly when seen through the eyes of a child. The excitement and anticipation, the simplicity in receiving, the earnestness in giving, the smiles, memories, and dreams.... This Christmas play with your children, read them stories, play games, create a gift together.... See Christmas again through the eyes of your child.

Sr. Ancilla Christine Hirsch, FSP

Pass the Present

This game is played like Hot Potato.

Supplies needed:

prize: miniature nativity (unbreakable)

several boxes of graduated sizes

several different colors of wrapping
   paper

ribbon   scissors   music

Directions:

Before the party:

1. Place the "prize" (miniature nativity) in a small box then wrap box with wrapping paper and tie ribbon around package.

2. Place that package into a larger box, wrap that box and tie ribbon around it.

3. Repeat process several times.

During the party:

1. Have guests sit on the floor, forming a large circle. Give the present to one guest to hold. You may need to explain the rules.

2. Start the music. As soon as the music begins, the person holding the present passes it to the guest on his/her right. He/she passes it to the person on his/her right, and so on.

3. When music stops, the person holding the present unwraps one layer.

4. Start the music again. Repeat the routine; the guest passes the present to the person to his/her right until the music stops and another layer of wrapping is removed.

5. This continues until the present is actually opened. The person who opens the final layer, keeps the "prize."

Reflection

"The Virgin today brings into the world
   the Eternal,
and the earth offers a cave to
   the Inaccessible."

Kontakion of Romanos the Melodist

Baby Jesus Birthday Party

Ten Questions

This is the perfect game for young detectives!

Before the party:

1. Read the Christmas story in Matthew 1:18–25 and 2:1–23, and Luke 1:26–80 and 2:1–40.

2. Based on the Scripture passages, write a list of persons, places, and things that relate to the birth of Jesus on note paper.

3. Write one person, place, or thing per note card. Make one note card for each guest.

4. Decorate the backs of these cards with symbols of the Advent or Christmas season.

During the party:

1. Explain the rules of the game. Have each guest pick one card from the deck. Remind them that they are not to show anyone the word on his/her card. The other players have to figure out what their word is by asking "Yes" or "No" questions.

2. Select one guest to be first.

3. The rest of the guests can ask a total of 10 questions in order to figure out the mystery person, place, or object. The first one to figure out what the word is, will be the next one to answer the questions. If no one figures out the word on the card after 10 questions have been asked, then the person holding the card shows the card to the guests.

Sample Questions:

Is your word a person?

Is the person a male? Female?

Is the person young? Old?

Is the person nice?

Is this person a relative of...?

Is your word a thing?

Is it a living thing?

Is it an animal?

Is it big?

Is it a non-living thing?

Is it found in the sky?

Is it found on the earth?

Can it hold something?

And other similar questions.

Words and Names you might want to include on your list:

Mary	Inn
Joseph	Straw
Jesus	Star
Zechariah	Shepherds
Elizabeth	Sheep
Simeon	Stable
Nazareth	Holy Night
Bethlehem	King
Herod	Donkey
Angels	Peace
Wise men	Good News
Manger	Joy
City of David	
Swaddling clothes	

Name That Tune!

Find out how well your guests know their Christmas songs with "Name That Tune!"

Before the party:

1. Write a list of titles for Christmas carols that you know.
2. Next to the titles, write the first lines of the carols.

During the party:

Supplies needed:

Paper

Pens

List of titles and first lines of songs

Directions:

1. Pass out a sheet of paper and a pen to each of your guests.

2. Have them write the numbers 1 through 12 on their paper.

3. Then read several words from the first line of a Christmas carol and ask them to write the title on their paper. Do this 12 times with 12 different songs.

4. To make the game more challenging, limit the number of words. You might start by giving the first 6 words of the first line. Do this for a few carol, then reduce the number of words to five, then four, etc.

5. The guest who correctly names the most titles wins the game. Variation: Play the first few measures of Christmas carols instead of reading the words.

Birthday Prayer to Jesus

After all of the games have been played, it's time for a piece of cake. So gather your guests, light the birthday candle, and explain the symbolism of the cake. Then say a special Birthday Prayer, sing Happy Birthday to Jesus, and enjoy a piece of cake with your guests! You may want to make copies of this prayer so that each guest has his/her own and then pray it together while gathered in front of a crèche.

Dear Jesus,

Thank you for coming to earth more than 2,000 years ago.

You taught the world about God.

You taught the world about peace.

You taught the world about faith, hope, and love.

YOU are the reason we're celebrating today.

Happy Birthday, dear Jesus!

We love you and praise you! Amen.

As mentioned earlier, the purpose for holding a Birthday Party for Jesus is actually two-fold. First, it helps children to celebrate in a special way the birthday of our Lord. Second, it fosters a spirit of caring and sharing with our brothers and sisters in Christ. By reaching out to others, even those we don't know by name, we teach our children to put their faith into action.

So when planning your Birthday Party for Jesus, allow plenty of time for "service projects."

Make sure you also allow time for your guests to make cards or write letters of encouragement for those who will be receiving these gifts of love. Simple messages like "God Bless You and Keep You!" or "From Our Kitchen to Yours!" or "God Cares and So Do We!" are messages the children might want to include. They can sign these cards and/or letters with something as simple as "From Someone Who Cares" or "From a Friend in Christ."

After the games have been played, Happy Birthday has been sung, and the cake has been served, it's time to work on your service projects!

If you've asked your guests to bring non-perishable gifts for a local food bank, then have your guests help separate the food into categories: fruits/veggies, canned meats/tuna, noodles/pasta/rice, etc. Then have a few guests write the categories on different grocery bags, and allow others to fill the bags with donated items. Together load the bags into a car.

If you've asked your guests to bring tubs of frosting and jars of sprinkles, gather your guests in your kitchen or dining room and get busy frosting cookies. Have plenty of counter space available where the cookies can sit until the frosting sets. Meanwhile, make the cards or write the letters to accompany the cookies!

If you've decided to support a nearby shelter with gifts of hats, gloves and scarves, then it's time to make the scarves! Before the party, purchase a few yards of 52 inch wide fleece fabric (or perhaps some of the guests could bring some fleece with them). Cut 6 scarves per yard. Each scarf measures 6 inches wide by 52 inches long.

These fleece scarves are a snap to make, even for non-craftsy, non-sewing guests! Simply have each guest cut "fringe" at the ends of your scarves and your scarves are ready to go! To make "fringe" have guests cut 1/4 inch wide strips 2 to 3 inches long at the ends of the pre-cut fleece scarves.

If you're donating gifts to a pregnancy center, then simply have your guests make cards or write letters that can be included with the gifts.

All gifts and cards or letters can be delivered after the party.

Christmas Season

The four weeks of Advent have led us to Christmas day. Our days of waiting are over! Christmas is finally here! This section offers family traditions and cultural customs as well as activities and prayers for the Christmas season which runs from Christmas day to Epiphany.

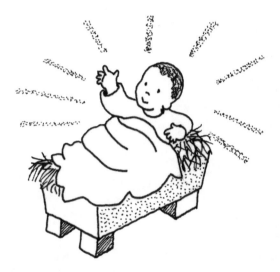

Season-at-a-Glance

Enjoy My Birthday

A Letter from Jesus

Illustrated by Tom Kinarney

Use this letter from Jesus and the accompanying activity for a few moments of quiet reflection with young ones as well as adults.

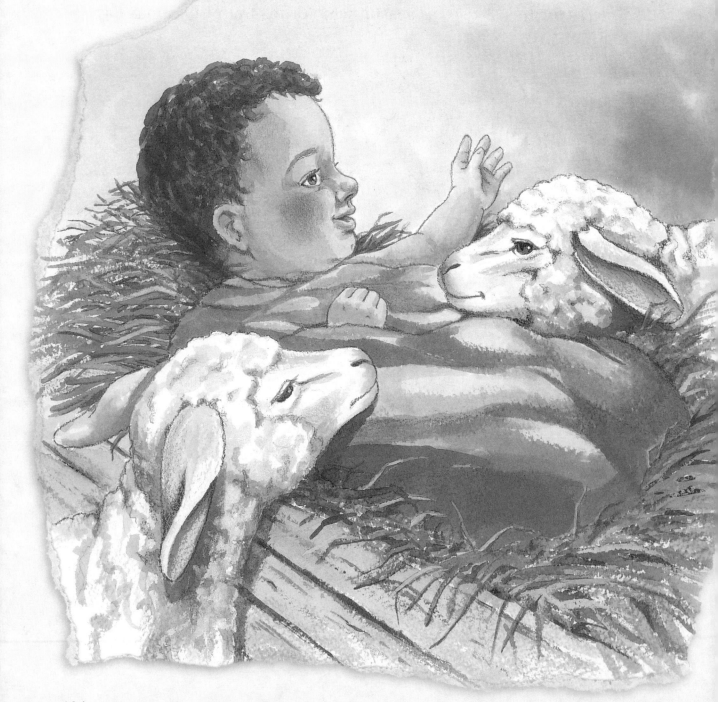

Dear Friend,

You must be getting excited about Christmas! What is your favorite part about the Advent-Christmas season? Is it family get-togethers? Or Christmas dinner? Or buying gifts for someone special and keeping it a surprise until Christmas Day? Or bringing a Christmas meal to a family who can't afford one? Or is it opening presents under the Christmas tree?

My Father knew how much you love presents. Actually, my Father was the first one to send a gift on the first Christmas morning! Do you remember that gift? The gift he wanted to give the world was his love, so he sent me to earth to show his love to everyone.

God knew that many people were fighting each other. He sent me to show people how to live in peace. If people learn from me, the world will be at peace.

God saw that people were lonely, so he sent me to show them that God cares about them and is with them all the time.

God saw that some people here didn't have food or any money, so he sent me not as a rich king, but as a member of a very poor family. He wanted poor people to know that he loved them. He also wants everyone to know that when they listen to what God says to them they will be first in his kingdom.

God wanted to give a present that was GOOD NEWS for the whole world. He wanted to tell the world God is LOVE. God is LOVE for you, all the time, in every place, where ever you go. I am always there.

When you need help, just call my name: Jesus. And I will be with you. I am with you all the time. You may not be able to see me, but if you pray, you will know that I am there.

Your Friend,
Jesus

A Quiet Place Meditation

Close your eyes.

Picture yourself on a hill outside Bethlehem. There are lots of stars in the sky, but one is especially bright.

You notice some activity around one of the stables. Go over and see what is happening.

There is a little crowd of shepherds. Gently push your way through and peek inside the stable.

There is a mother. She is very beautiful. And a tiny baby lying in a manger.

One of the shepherds turns to you and says, "The angels told us that this baby has come to bring us peace."

Even though you have no real gift with you, walk up real close to the manger in which Jesus is laid.

See Mary nod at you. Pick Jesus up and hold him close to your heart. What does he say to you?

The Story of Christmas

Begin your family Christmas celebrations by lighting the Christmas candle (page 84) and reading the story of the first Christmas.

Though children hear the Christmas Gospel read at Mass on Christmas Eve or at one of the Masses on Christmas day, it is helpful to re-read the Gospel with your children at home after the gifts have been opened. Prior to opening gifts, young children can be so overcome with the excitement and anticipation of opening the presents that they find it difficult to focus on the readings at Mass. A perfect time to reflect on the Christmas Gospel is when the family gathers around the table for a meal on Christmas day.

Try sharing the Word of the Lord with your family this year before enjoying your Christmas feast. Read the story of the first Christmas slowly, with awe in your voice. Help your children understand that Christmas is all about God's gift of Love.

The Birth of Jesus–Luke 2:1–7

About that time Emperor Augustus gave orders for the names of all the people to be listed in record books. These first records were made when Quirinius was governor of Syria. Everyone had to go to their own hometown to be listed. So Joseph had to leave Nazareth in Galilee and go to Bethlehem in Judea. Long ago Bethlehem had been King David's hometown, and Joseph went there because he was from David's family.

Mary was engaged to Joseph and traveled with him to Bethlehem. She was soon going to have a baby, and while they were there, she gave birth to her first-born son. She dressed him in baby clothes and laid him on a bed of hay because there was no room for them in the inn.

The Shepherds—Luke 2:8–20

That night in the fields near Bethlehem some shepherds were guarding their sheep. All at once an angel came down to them from the Lord, and the brightness of the Lord's glory flashed around them. The shepherds were frightened. But the angel said, "Don't be afraid! I have good news for you, which will make everyone happy. This very day in King David's hometown a Savior was born for you. He is Christ the Lord. You will know who he is, because you will find him dressed in baby clothes and lying on a bed of hay."

Suddenly many other angels came down from heaven and joined in praising God. They said, "Praise God in heaven! Peace on earth to everyone who pleases God."

After the angels had left and gone back to heaven, the shepherds said to each other, "Let's go to Bethlehem and see what the Lord has told us about." They hurried off and found Mary and Joseph, and they saw the baby lying on a bed of hay.

When the shepherds saw Jesus, they told his parents what the angel had said about him.

Everyone listened and was surprised. But Mary kept thinking about all this and wondering what it meant.

As the shepherds returned to their sheep, they were praising God and saying wonderful things about him. Everything they had seen and heard was just as the angel had said.

During the lengthy season of Christmas consider using any of these prayers before family meals or during family prayer times. Photocopy this page with enough copies for your whole family and guests to use.

Christmas Prayer

Sweet Jesus, today we celebrate your birthday—we've waited all of Advent for this special day to come! As we celebrate your birthday, we say a special "THANK YOU!" for your tremendous gift of love. And we pray that you will continue to help us share your love with others so they, too, will come to know you and love you. We are so thankful that you are with us. We love you, Jesus, Emmanuel! Amen.

Prayer to the Holy Family

Dear Jesus, Mary and Joseph, as we celebrate the feast of the Holy Family, we thank you for your example of family and love. Please help us follow your example— help us to be loving, forgiving, and kind. Please help us to live in peace with each other and to carry that peace to all people. Amen.

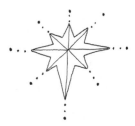

Epiphany Prayer

Lord Jesus, today we celebrate the day the wise men honored you as the newborn King of kings. They gave you some of the world's finest gifts, gifts of gold, frankincense and myrrh. The wise men followed the star to the place where you were found. They never doubted their journey. They never doubted the star. They followed faithfully its radiant light. Help us to be like the wise men. Help us to follow the light of your Word. Amen.

Reflection

The hidden gesture of the three kings bending down to the child and offering him mysterious gifts is a constant invitation for us to enter that lost dwelling, to lower our heads at the nativity in Bethlehem, and to accomplish in the heart of the world—even if the world does not want either to see it or to know it—these acts of love, of praise, and of faithful adherence that will manifest who it is that we have found. Love works quietly to sabotage the world's refusal to welcome its Savior.

Erasmo Leiva-Merikakis

Christmas Morning Pancakes

With the help of a "spouted" measuring cup, you and your family can make pancakes in the shape of hearts, shepherd's staffs, the Bethlehem star, or Christmas trees. Simply pour the batter onto the hot griddle in the shape of symbols of the Christmas season!

Supplies needed:

"spouted" measuring cup
medium sized mixing bowl
mixer or wire whisk
griddle   spatula

Ingredients:

1 egg
2 tbsp. of cooking oil
1 cup of milk
1 tbsp. sugar
1/2 tsp. salt
1 cup flour
1 tsp. baking powder
1 tsp. baking soda
margarine for greasing griddle or non-stick cooking spray

Directions:

1. In a medium mixing bowl, beat egg with wire whisk or mixer.

2. Add oil and milk. Stir until ingredients are well blended.

3. Add the rest of the ingredients in the order in which they are listed. Mix until batter is smooth.

4. Coat griddle with thin layer of margarine or non-stick cooking spray.

5. Pour batter onto hot griddle, forming shapes as you go.

6. When batter bubbles, flip pancakes over. (They should be golden brown.) Wait a few minutes and flip again. Serve Christmas Pancakes with butter, jam, honey or syrup.

7. Serve with eggs, bacon, and a colorful Christmas fruit salad (page 110) and Sunrise Punch (page 110).

Makes 18 medium-sized pancakes or 4 servings.

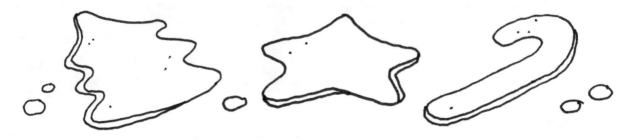

Colorful Christmas Fruit Salad

Add color to your Christmas breakfast with this refreshing fruit salad.

Supplies needed:

medium-sized clear glass bowl
can opener   knife
spoon   colander
plastic bowl

Ingredients:

4 kiwi
2 cans pineapple chunks
2 cans mandarin oranges
1 small jar maraschino cherries
2 cups miniature marshmallows

Directions:

1. Peel and slice two kiwi. Layer kiwi on the bottom of a medium-sized clear glass bowl.

2. Open one can of pineapple chunks. Empty can into colander placed over a plastic bowl. Drain and save juice to add to your favorite fruit punch later on. Spoon pineapple chunks over kiwi.

3. Open one can of mandarin oranges. Drain juice. Spoon oranges over pineapple chunks.

4. Sprinkle one cup of miniature marshmallows over fruit.

5. Repeat steps one through four and then top salad with maraschino cherries. Chil' until ready to serve.

Number of servings: 12. Serving Size: 3/4 cup

Christmas Sunrise Punch

Supplies needed:

wooden skewers for fruit kabobs

Ingredients:

1 tbsp. frozen cranberry juice cocktail concentrate
1 tbsp. pineapple juice (saved from *Colorful Christmas Fruit Salad*)
1 cup orange juice
5 fresh cranberries
3 pineapple chunks

Directions:

1. Drop a spoonful of frozen cranberry juice cocktail concentrate into glass tumbler.

2. Pour a tablespoon of pineapple juice into tumbler.

3. Fill tumbler with orange juice.

4. Spear cranberries and pineapple chunks onto wooden skewer and stir ingredients.

Traditions create memories. Memories enrich our lives. Traditions help us pass on valuable lessons to our children and our children's children.

Sharing the Christmas Wafer

Many families share beautiful Christmas customs, which have been passed down from generation to generation. Among these treasured traditions is the customary Christmas Eve or Christmas day feast.

For many families of Slovak or Polish heritage, the *oplatka* or Christmas wafer is an important part of their Christmas Eve feast. *Oplatka* is a piece of unleavened bread imprinted with the nativity scene or another Christmas scene such as the wise men enroute to the newborn King of kings.

Christmas wafers, or *oplatky*, are usually rectangular in shape and taste like the host we receive for Eucharist. They are blessed, but they are not consecrated.

The word *oplatka* is derived from the Latin word *oblata* which means offering. The Latin word *oblatum* means holy bread.

When the Christmas Eve feast is about to begin, the wafer is broken by the head of the household and shared with each member of the family. As the head of the household offers a piece of the wafer to each person who is present, he or she embraces them and asks for forgiveness for any hurt he or she may have caused during the year. Others in the family also ask for forgiveness. It is a time for reconciliation, a sign of peace. It is a fitting custom to include in our celebrations of the birth of Jesus, the Prince of Peace.

To find out more about optlatky *visit the following website: Oplatki On Line http://www.iarelative.com/xmas/oplatki.htm.*

Reflection

As day swallows day in our Advent rush, we suddenly arrive at Christmas and discover that Christ has surprised us from behind. Sitting before a crackling fire or a twinkling tree we discover from the deepest, most personal parts of our being that Christmas has happened. In all the rush, Christ was being born in our own lives. G. K. Chesterton says, "It is as if we had found an inner room in the very heart of our own house, which we had never suspected; and seen a light from within." In making ourselves more and more at home in this room, which gradually is revealed to us, each Advent becomes more simple. As the years pass, Christ does invade our lives—simplifying, inviting, transforming.

Sr. Kathryn James Hermes, FSP

The Mexican Piñata

The Mexicans have several Christmas traditions which are quickly becoming part of Christmas festivities in parishes across the country. Las Posadas is a religious and social celebration which commemorates Mary and Joseph's cold and difficult journey from Nazareth to Bethlehem in search of shelter. Mexican festivities are also known for the piñata.

Supplies needed:

white glue (about 1 cup)

bowl	craft knife
a balloon	newspaper
needle	tissue paper
white paper	paint

masking tape

candies or small treats and toys

thread to hang the piñata

Directions:

1. Cover your work area with newspaper.

2. Blow the balloon up and tie it shut. Pour about a cup of white glue into a bowl and add enough water to make it the consistency of cream.

3. Take the newspaper and tear it up into strips that are about 1 inch or less in width and about 6 to 8 inches long. Drag them through the glue-paste and plaster the balloon with the gluey strips. You will need to build up about five or six layers of paper. (Hint: To make sure you finish each layer, use black and white news print for one layer and then color comics for the next.)

4. Once the five layers are ready, let the piñata dry overnight. Take a pin and push it through the papier-mâché to pop the balloon inside.

5. In order to get the candy or small treats into the center of the papier-mâché piñata, use a craft knife to cut a small circle out of one end and pour in the candy. Then tape the small piece back on.

6. Using white paper put on another layer of glue and paper. Let it dry overnight before decorating the piñata with tissue paper and paint.

7. Use a needle and thread to string up the piñata and hang it from the ceiling. When you're ready, have people take turns whacking it with a stick while blindfolded. When the piñata breaks, everyone scrambles for the prizes!

Epiphany Customs

The twelve days of Christmas stretch between December 25 and January 6, which is the Feast of the Epiphany. Epiphany is the last day of the Christmas season and one of the greatest feasts of the liturgical year. It celebrates the Magi from the East who came in search of the new King. Tradition has given us a few details about these respected wise men from Persia: there were three of them, they were kings, and their names were Gaspar, Melchior, and Balthasar. The figurines of the three kings, which have not yet been placed in the crèche, begin a 12-day journey toward the Christ Child. They can be placed at a distance across the room and moved toward the crèche day by day, until finally on January 6 they are placed in the crèche. Although there are traditional Epiphany observances from countries around the world, Germany is most noted for its traditional festivities to celebrate this day.

Reflection

"If God wants to meet us as a man—indeed, as a child—then we too must reach out to him. We must set out on the road like the shepherds of Bethlehem, like the wise men from the East."

John Paul II

Solemn Blessing of the Home

In Germany, every year around Epiphany, children used to go from house to house dressed up as three kings to sing and collect a special offering for poor children. Before they would leave they would mark the doorways of the house with a blessing which would remain on the doorframe for the rest of the year. In the Middle Ages the family would process through the house with the father carrying charcoal and a child carrying incense. Each room of the house would be blessed with holy water. Holy water can easily be obtained from your parish church and kept in a clean bottle.

1. Create by hand or through computer art several small signs which can be taped to the doorways leading outside of the house. The sign should include the initials of the Magi together with the year and several crosses that connect all of the letters and numbers, for example, A.D. 20+C+M+B+04 which stands for "Anno Domini 2004—Caspar, Melchior, Balthasar" (although some believe that these initials stood for the Latin phrase: *Christus Mansionem Benedicat*, which means "Christ bless this house").

2. Obtain a bottle of holy water from your parish church.

   Invite a parish priest over for dinner to solemnly bless your home, or simply gather the

A.D. 20+C+M+B+04

family together and ask for God's blessings on your family and home.

3. Together go into each room of your house. Name what happens in that room, for example, sleeping, sharing family meals, watching videos, surfing the net, doing homework, etc. Ask God to bless those who live in these rooms with pure minds and loving hearts and the wisdom to follow God's will in all that they say, whether they're involved in work, rest, or play, and to protect the whole family from evil and sin when you are in that room.

Sprinkle the room with holy water.

4. Tape the signs to the doorframes of doors that lead out of the house. This tradition of blessing doorways symbolizes the family's commitment to welcome Christ into their homes on a daily basis throughout the year.

King's Cake

The King's Cake or Epiphany cake varies from country to country, but its one common characteristic is a coin or small figurine placed inside the batter before baking. The person whose piece of cake has this object gets to be "king" for the day. The custom in some European countries was to have a bean and a pea in the cake: the man who got the bean would be king and the woman who got the pea would be queen.

Reflection

Christmas can also be tinged with the sadness, depression, or pain that signals unresolved losses, unfinished grieving, or the incongruence of Christmas dreams and realities. Blues may arise from the stress of the extra demands made upon us. What can we do:

Acknowledge and explore losses and grief. Seek to come a step closer to resolution. Ask help if necessary.

If gift-giving is becoming too great a burden, think about other ways to express your love for family and friends, or other ways to organize your gift buying. Perhaps talk it over with your family.

Make a tradition of attending a special Christmas liturgy each year.

Surround yourself with supportive people and minimize time spent with negative people (even if they are family members).

Try to recognize and reframe unrealistic expectations.

Get extra rest and exercise regularly.

Create new ways to celebrate, or set aside time just for yourself to experience the Christmas season in a way that is more meaningful.

Enjoy activities that are free.

Do something for someone else.

Keep to your budget.

Don't overindulge in holiday treats.

Give priority to gifts that can't be bought.

Reproducible Pages

Reproducible Pages-at-a-glance

Name _____

Advent Wreath Word Search

Directions: The words in bold print are hidden in the word search below. See how many words you can find!

Advent is a time of waiting, a time for **hoping**, a time for **preparing** our **hearts** and **homes** for the coming **celebration** of **Christmas**. For many families, the Advent **wreath** is a **symbol** for the season. It helps them mark their days of waiting. The wreath forms a **circle**, the symbol for eternal life. The **candles** remind us of **Jesus**, the Light of the World. **Purple**, a symbol for **royalty**, reminds us of **Christ**, the King of kings. **Pink** is a sign of **joy** and **hope**. It reminds us that Christmas is almost here!

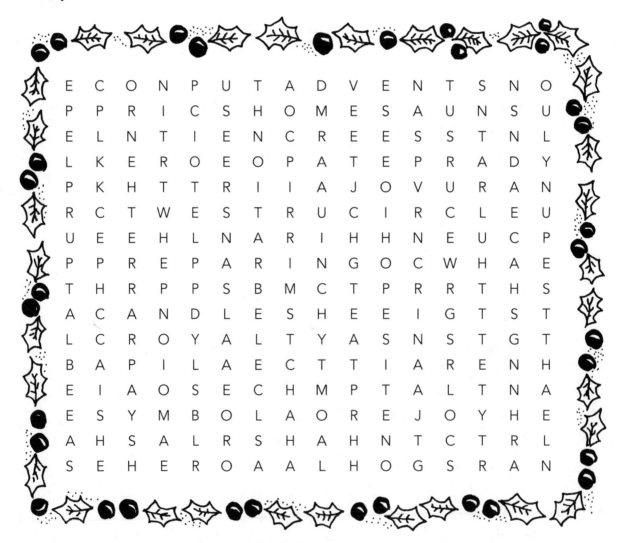

```
E  C  O  N  P  U  T  A  D  V  E  N  T  S  N  O
P  P  R  I  C  S  H  O  M  E  S  A  U  N  S  U
E  L  N  T  I  E  N  C  R  E  E  S  S  T  N  L
L  K  E  R  O  E  O  P  A  T  E  P  R  A  D  Y
P  K  H  T  T  R  I  I  A  J  O  V  U  R  A  N
R  C  T  W  E  S  T  R  U  C  I  R  C  L  E  U
U  E  E  H  L  N  A  R  I  H  H  N  E  U  C  P
P  P  R  E  P  A  R  I  N  G  O  C  W  H  A  E
T  H  R  P  P  S  B  M  C  T  P  R  R  T  H  S
A  C  A  N  D  L  E  S  H  E  E  I  G  T  S  T
L  C  R  O  Y  A  L  T  Y  A  S  N  S  T  G  T
B  A  P  I  L  A  E  C  T  T  I  A  R  E  N  H
E  I  A  O  S  E  C  H  M  P  T  A  L  T  N  A
E  S  Y  M  B  O  L  A  O  R  E  J  O  Y  H  E
A  H  S  A  L  R  S  H  A  H  N  T  C  T  R  L
S  E  H  E  R  O  A  A  L  H  O  G  S  R  A  N
```

The Advent–Christmas Book

Name _____

A Special Announcement!

The prophet Isaiah said:
"A virgin will have a baby boy and...."

Directions: Follow the arrows that lead to boxes with matching letters. Fill in the letters to discover the rest of Isaiah's message.

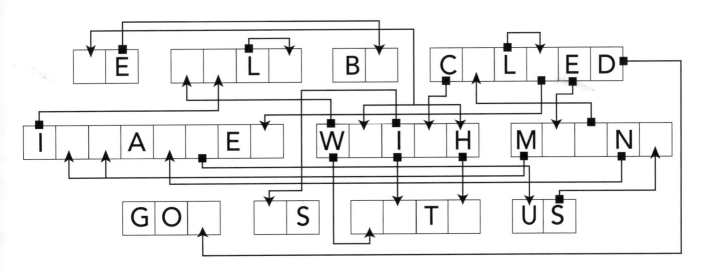

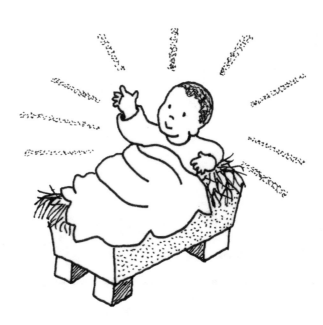

Name _____

John the Baptist Word Scramble

The prophet Isaiah said that someone would prepare the way of the Lord. That someone was John the Baptist.

Directions: Unscramble the words below to find out what John the Baptist shouted in the desert (Mk 1:1–3). Then color the page.

TGE   HET   AROD   DEARY

___ ___ ___   ___ ___ ___   ___ ___ ___ ___   ___ ___ ___ ___ ___

ROF   EHT   DROL!   KEAM

___ ___ ___   ___ ___ ___   ___ ___ ___ ___   ___ ___ ___ ___

A   TTHIASGR   TAPH

___   ___ ___ ___ ___ ___ ___ ___ ___   ___ ___ ___ ___

OFR   IHM

___ ___ ___   ___ ___ ___ .

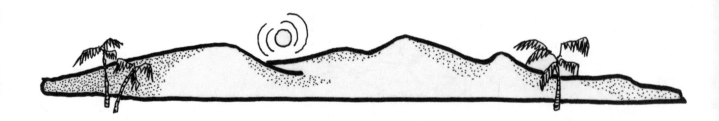

The Advent–Christmas Book

Name _____

Directions: Color the picture below. Write a short prayer on the back thanking God for the gift of Jesus!

The Angel Gabriel and Mary

Gabriel told Mary, "Don't be afraid! God is pleased with you, and you will have a son. His name will be Jesus" (cf. Lk 1:30–31).

Name _____

Mary Obeys

Directions: Follow the arrows and fill in the matching boxes to discover what Mary said to the angel Gabriel when he told her she would be the mother of Jesus. Then color in the picture.

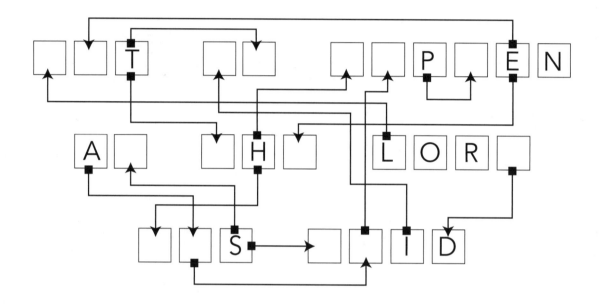

The Advent–Christmas Book

Name _____

The Angel Gabriel and Joseph

The angel visited Joseph in a dream. He told Joseph that Mary would have a baby boy and that they should name him Jesus. He also told him why they should name him Jesus. Find out what the angel said by solving the puzzle below.

Directions: Choose from the following words:

from, he, his, people, save, sins, their, will.

Figure out which words go on which blanks. Write the words on the blanks then color the picture below.

— —   — — — — —   — — — — —   — — —

— — — — —   — — — —   — — — — —

— — — — — .

Name _____

Canticle of Mary

A canticle is a sacred song or chant. A part of the Canticle of Mary is found in the maze below. When Mary's cousin Elizabeth realized that Mary would be the Mother of God, Mary responded with this canticle or song of praise.

Directions: Wind through the maze to discover what Mary said. Write out the words in order at the bottom of the page. Read the rest of the canticle in Luke 1:46–55.

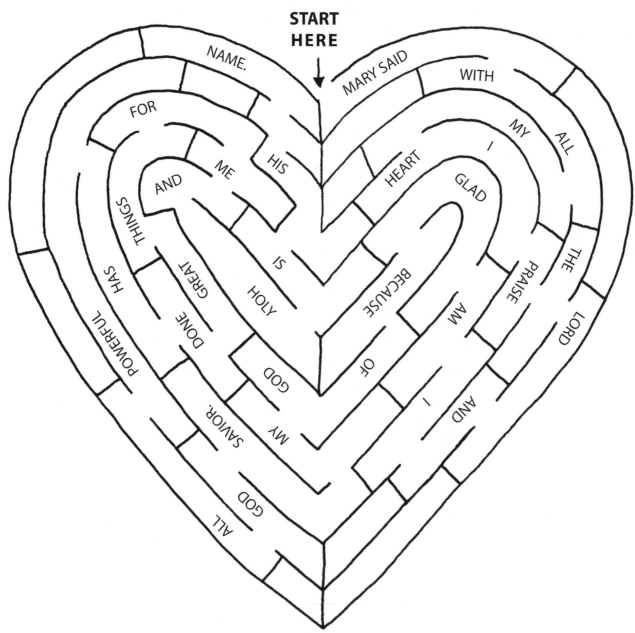

The Advent–Christmas Book

Name _____

Christmas Word Search

Directions: See how many of the following words you can find in the word search below.

angels	frankincense	hope	manger	Father Forever
baby	Gabriel	hymns	Mary	shepherds
Bethlehem	gifts	Jesus	Messiah	swaddling clothes
Christ	glad tidings	Joseph	myrrh	Wonder Counselor
Emmanuel	God Hero	Judea	praise	Prince of Peace
faith	gold	king	star	
wise men	Holy Spirit	love	virgin	

```
Y T O I S E M E P R A I S E A S J O S E P H P
F S T A R W S E M D R R W I S E M E N H E M R
A R H E M L A I S M A B L O V E N Y I H A E I
T H A A H M S D M S A L G N H A R H Y M N S N
H L E N Y A R W D O I N G S S A S W A N G A C
E I N R K A E F A L R A U S M Y N O P A E M E
R T R B S I I D L D I P H E G A B R I E L O O
F H R E F G N S U T D N O U L G G S N S S S F
O I E T D S I C S J O L G F A I T H W P E U P
R E G H L L G I E E N U I C O S G I F T S S E
E G N L O M R G A N I M L N L H E P O H G E A
V E A E G H I I B G S A N G G O I C N U O J C
E N M H C S V I S R I E H O L Y T K I N G M E
R Y E E B A B Y S H E P H E R D S H O E G N G
B Y O M L H O L Y S P I R I T D E W E N E C N
U E H S U E E H S G N I D I T D A L G S I H J
W O N D E R C O U N S E L O R L O R E H D O G
```

Name _____

Mary and Joseph

Joseph and Mary traveled nearly 80 miles from Nazareth to Bethlehem where Jesus was born.

Directions: Find the path that leads Mary and Joseph from Nazareth to Bethlehem. What kinds of things do you think Mary and Joseph were able to take with them on their journey?

The Advent–Christmas Book

Name _____

The Holy Family

Directions: Color the picture of the Holy Family. On the back of the paper write a simple prayer to the Holy Family.

Name _____

Your "Holy" Family

Every family can be a "holy" family by living according to God's Word.

Directions: Draw and color a picture of your "holy" family below.

The Advent–Christmas Book

Name _____

Names for Jesus

Directions: See how many different names for Jesus you can find hidden in the puzzle below. Which one do you like best? Write a sentence about why you like it best.

Name _____

The Angel and the Shepherds

Directions: Use the code below to find out what the angel said to the shepherds on the night that Jesus was born.

___ ___   ___ ___ ___   ___ ___
3,7 5,10   1,7 2,9 4,8   1,10 5,6

___ ___ ___ ___ ___ ___
3,10 4,6 2,7 2,8 2,6 4,9

	6	7	8	9	10
1	C	N	P	M	B
2	I	R	A	O	E
3	M	D	J	G	A
4	F	S	T	D	L
5	E	C	R	P	O

The Advent–Christmas Book

Name _____

The Shepherds

An angel told shepherds that the Savior was born in King David's hometown. The angel told them to look for the sign—a baby wrapped in swaddling clothes and lying in a manger. The shepherds hurried to Bethlehem to find Jesus.

Directions: Find the path that leads the shepherds to Jesus. If you were one of the shepherds, what would you say to Mary, Joseph, and Baby Jesus? Turn the paper over and write down at least two things you would say to them.

Name _____

The Angels' Song of Praise

The angels sang a beautiful song when Jesus was born.

Directions: Use the code below to find out what the angels said. What's your favorite song to sing to Jesus?

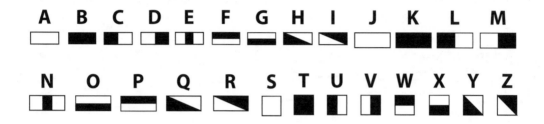

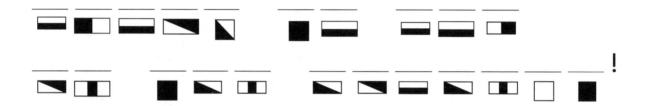

My favorite song to sing to Jesus is _____ .

The Advent–Christmas Book

Name _____

The Light

Directions: Follow the arrows that lead to boxes with matching letters. Fill in the letters to discover this familiar Advent verse found in the book of the prophet Isaiah.

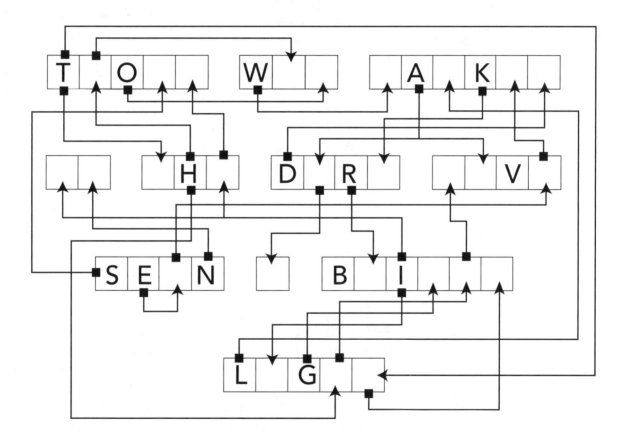

Name _____

The Three Wise Men

The three wise men followed the star to Bethlehem to find the new-born King of kings.

Directions: Find the path that leads to Bethlehem. At the bottom of the maze write the three gifts they brought to Jesus.

Name _____

God's Gifts to You

God has blessed each of us with many wonderful gifts.

Directions: Draw some of the gifts God has given to you. Then color the "frame" of presents.

Name _____

Your Gifts to God

The wise men gave Jesus precious gifts of gold, frankincense, and myrrh.

Directions: In each of the packages write or draw pictures of the gifts you can give Jesus.

　　　　　　　　　　　　　　　The Advent–Christmas Book

Name _____

Let's Celebrate!

Directions: Unscramble the letters below to discover the Bible verse taken from Psalm 98:5–6.

Make __ __ __ __ __ for him on __ __ __ __ __ .
S M U I C   S H P A R

Play __ __ __ __ __ __ __ __ __ melodies!
A B E F I U T U L

Sound the __ __ __ __ __ __ __ __ and
S T R U M T E P

__ __ __ __ __ and __ __ __ __ __ __ __ __ __
N O R S H   B R A T E E E L C

with joyful __ __ __ __ __
G O N S S

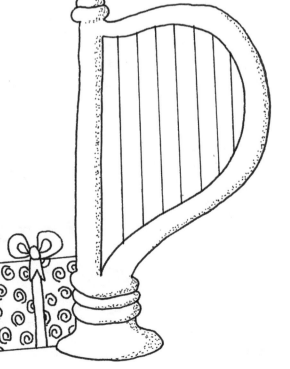

Name _____

Joyful Prayers

This "Tip for Living" is found in the Bible in First Thessalonians 5:16–17.

Directions: Use the code below to find out what we should be doing while we are waiting for Jesus to come again.

The Advent–Christmas Book

Name _____

Peace and Justice

The Lord will bring about justice and peace in every nation on earth, like flowers blooming in a garden (Is 61:11).

Directions: Color the picture.

Name _____

Peace

Directions: Follow the lines below to find out how to say "PEACE" in 15 languages.

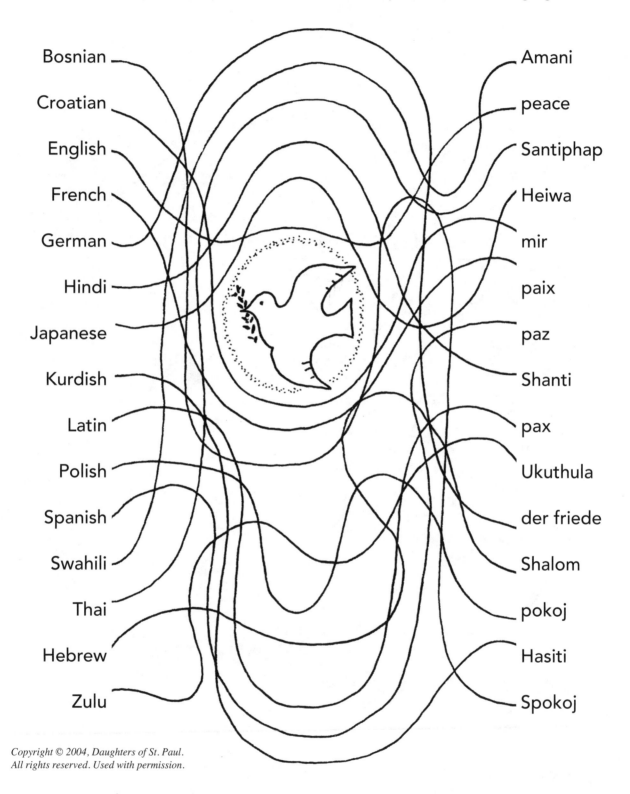

Bosnian

Croatian

English

French

German

Hindi

Japanese

Kurdish

Latin

Polish

Spanish

Swahili

Thai

Hebrew

Zulu

Amani

peace

Santiphap

Heiwa

mir

paix

paz

Shanti

pax

Ukuthula

der friede

Shalom

pokoj

Hasiti

Spokoj

The Advent–Christmas Book

p. 116

```
E C O N P U T A D V E N T S N O
P P R I C S H O M E S A U N S U
E L N T I E N C R E E S S T N L
L K E R O E O P A T E P R A D Y
P K H T T R I I A J O V U R A N
R C T W E S T R U C I R C L E U
U E E H L N A R I H H N E U C P
P P R E P A R I N G O C W H A E
T H R P P S B M C T P R R T H S
A C A N D L E S H E E I G T S T
L C R O Y A L T Y A S N S T G T
B A P I L A E C T T I A R E N H
E I A O S E C H M P T A L T N A
E S Y M B O L A O R E J O Y H E
A H S A L R S H A H N T C T R L
S E H E R O A A L H O G S R A N
```

p. 117

He will be called Emmanuel which means God is with us.

p. 118

Get the road ready for the Lord! Make a straight path for him.

p. 120

Let it happen as the Lord has said.

p. 121

He will save his people from their sins.

p. 122

Mary said With all my heart I praise the Lord, and I am glad because of God, my Savior. God All-Powerful has done great things for me and his name is holy.

p. 123

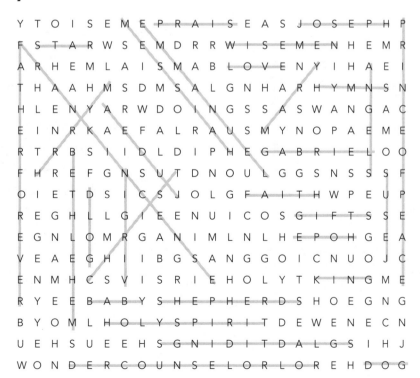

```
Y T O I S E M E P R A I S E A S J O S E P H P
F S T A R W S E M D R R W I S E M E N H E M R
A R H E M L A I S M A B L O V E N Y I H A E I
T H A A H M S D M S A L G N H A R H Y M N S N
H L E N Y A R W D O I N G S S A S W A N G A C
E I N R K A E F A L R A U S M Y N O P A E M E
R T R B S I I D L D I P H E G A B R I E L O O
F H R E F G N S U T D N O U L G G S N S S S F
O I E T D S I C S J O L G F A I T H W P E U P
R E G H L L G I E E N U I C O S G I F T S S E
E G N L O M R G A N I M L N L H E P O H G E A
V E A E G H I I B G S A N G G O I C N U O J C
E N M H C S V I S R I E H O L Y T K I N G M E
R Y E E B A B Y S H E P H E R D S H O E G N G
B Y O M L H O L Y S P I R I T D E W E N E C N
U E H S U E E H S G N I D I T D A L G S I H J
W O N D E R C O U N S E L O R L O R E H D O G
```

ANSWERS

p. 124

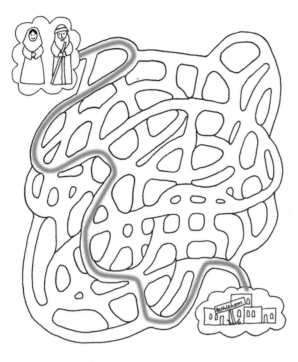

p. 128

Do not be afraid.

p. 129

p. 130

Glory to God in the highest.

p. 127

The Good Shepherd	God Hero
Father Forever	Prince of Peace
Son of God	Our Lord and Savior
Christ	Lamb of God
The Messiah	Emmanuel
Wonder Counselor	King of kings

p. 131

Those who walked in the dark have seen a bright light.

p. 132

p. 135

Make music for him on harps. Play beautiful melodies! Sound the trumpets and horns and celebrate with joyful songs.

p. 136

Always be joyful, never stop praying.

The Advent–Christmas Book

Experience True Adventure and Heroism!

Blessed Teresa of Calcutta
Missionary of Charity

avich, SND

Saint Thérèse of Lisieux
The Way of Love

by Mary Kathleen Glavich, SND

Saint Pio of Pietrelcina
Rich in Love
by Eileen Dunn Bertanzet

Saint Ignatius of Loyola
For the Greater Glory of God

by Donna William Giaimo, FSP and
Patricia Edward Jablonski, FSP

The Saints Live and Breathe
Again in These Stories
You Won't Want to Put Down!

Pauline
BOOKS & MEDIA

The Daughters of St. Paul operate book and media centers at the following addresses. Visit, call or write the one nearest you today, or find us on the World Wide Web, www.pauline.org

CALIFORNIA	3908 Sepulveda Blvd, Culver City, CA 90230	310-397-8676
	5945 Balboa Avenue, San Diego, CA 92111	858-565-9181
	46 Geary Street, San Francisco, CA 94108	415-781-5180
FLORIDA	145 S.W. 107th Avenue, Miami, FL 33174	305-559-6715
HAWAII	1143 Bishop Street, Honolulu, HI 96813	808-521-2731
	Neighbor Islands call:	866-521-2731
ILLINOIS	172 North Michigan Avenue, Chicago, IL 60601	312-346-4228
LOUISIANA	4403 Veterans Memorial Blvd, Metairie, LA 70006	504-887-7631
MASSACHUSETTS	885 Providence Hwy, Dedham, MA 02026	781-326-5385
MISSOURI	9804 Watson Road, St. Louis, MO 63126	314-965-3512
NEW JERSEY	561 U.S. Route 1, Wick Plaza, Edison, NJ 08817	732-572-1200
NEW YORK	150 East 52nd Street, New York, NY 10022	212-754-1110
	78 Fort Place, Staten Island, NY 10301	718-447-5071
PENNSYLVANIA	9171-A Roosevelt Blvd, Philadelphia, PA 19114	215-676-9494
SOUTH CAROLINA	243 King Street, Charleston, SC 29401	843-577-0175
TENNESSEE	4811 Poplar Avenue, Memphis, TN 38117	901-761-2987
TEXAS	114 Main Plaza, San Antonio, TX 78205	210-224-8101
VIRGINIA	1025 King Street, Alexandria, VA 22314	703-549-3806
CANADA	3022 Dufferin Street, Toronto, Ontario, Canada M6B 3T5	416-781-9131
	1155 Yonge Street, Toronto, Ontario, Canada M4T 1W2	416-934-3440

¡También somos su fuente para libros, videos y música en español!

144   *blank (last page)*